THE CREATIVE EDGE OF AMERICAN
PROTESTANTISM

THE CREATIVE EDGE OF AMERICAN PROTESTANTISM

Earl H. Brill

THE SEABURY PRESS · NEW YORK

TO RUTH

_____

PREFACE

I SHOULD LIKE to acknowledge my indebtedness to the Danforth Foundation, which provided a year of freedom from professional duties, thereby making it possible for me to undertake this study. At the same time, I would thank most heartily those colleagues who have so willingly offered me their guidance and assistance. Kenneth Condit and Charles McLaughlin read parts of the manuscript and made valuable suggestions. Margaret Guenther's sharp eye and keen judgment saved me from many stylistic errors. Finally, of course, I owe to my wife a special debt that I can never repay, for her cheerful cooperation and encouragement throughout the whole process of study and writing.

E.H.B.

CONTENTS

INTRODUCTION

THE DECADE following the close of World War II saw a dramatic increase of interest in religion in America. Church membership climbed to new heights. Religious books and movies enjoyed unprecedented popularity. For a time it looked as though a whole generation whose parents had rejected organized religion was being won back to the churches.

But this religious revival soon began to betray signs of disquieting superficiality. Though large organization churches were developed, most of them showed little evidence that they knew why they were in business. Intelligent, resourceful, and willing people were lured into the churches only to be nurtured there with a nonjudgmental, family-oriented, neighborly kind of piety that seldom moved beyond the confines of the local housing development. As time went on, the men became caught up in more important concerns, and the churches gradually found themselves ministering, for the most part, to the women, children, and old folks, who have been relegated to the fringes of modern society.

Today there are signs that the churches are about to break out of their cultural ghetto. They are becoming aware of a whole world of issues to which the Christian faith is relevant. The churches have begun to recognize that social change is abroad in the land, and they are showing a gratifying readiness to move into the center of social change.

Actually this new situation represents a return to what Winthrop Hudson has called "the great tradition of the American Churches. . . ." [1] For throughout American history, it has been the glory of the churches to have been related closely and directly to American society. On the other hand, it has been their shame that this relationship has not been more creative and fruitful. Any understanding of the present role of the church in American society must be grounded in a knowledge of that "great tradition." Fortunately, the labor of a generation of scholars has made it possible for us to see that tradition in new perspective. Both churchly and secular historians have been reassessing, with a new openness and sensitivity, the mutual interactions of church and culture. As a result, the effect of the American environment on Christianity can be seen with some clarity.

The present study is an attempt to make use of the historical perspective to shed light on some of the significant social and political issues which the American churches face today. The result is a topical survey which is meant to be selective and interpretive rather than comprehensive. The actual historical periods covered will vary with the subject under discussion. The church-state issue, for example, is traced back to its colonial origins, whereas the chapter on international relations begins around the turn of this century. The discussion has been limited to Protestantism because Protestantism in America shows a fairly consistent line of historical development. And despite its lack of precision, we shall use the term "Protestantism" in the manner of popular speech.

Within the broad spectrum of what passes for Protestantism in the United States, we shall place our emphasis on those areas where change has occurred. The issues discussed have been selected in order to show how much change has taken place both in society at large and in the Protestant position within society. Lest this approach seem to exaggerate the scope and momentum of change, it might be worth-while to add that the large mass of Protestants have remained within the boundaries, so to speak. They have gone along with change, but not always willingly. They have resisted change, but not always vigorously. Yet it is only by focusing on the creative edge of change that the story can be told, for it is there that the magnitude and direction of change can best be seen.

The concern in the pages that follow will be less with theological than with social change. The creative edge of Protestantism can be identified as that segment of the Protestant community which, at any given time, is most aware of the realities of the social situation and which seeks to bring to bear upon that situation the insights and concerns of the Christian faith. American Protestantism has been most vital and incisive when it has retained its theologico-biblical grounding while preserving a genuine concern for society.

When its concern for society is lost, religion degenerates into sentimental piety or narrow dogmatic exclusiveness. When its theological grounding is lost, the church is easily led to sell out to the culture by bestowing its benediction indiscriminately on whatever movements and forces prevail in the society. American Protestantism has been subject to both distortions. It has not found it easy to maintain that sensitive balance of theological integrity and openness to new situations.

Indeed, the attitude of the churches toward social and political questions has been conditioned by the nature of their place in American society. Church historians have distinguished three epochs in which that position differed markedly.[2] In the early period, just after the Revolution, the Congregational and Episcopal churches, which had enjoyed government support, were left weak and demoralized. The newer free churches, such as the Baptist and Methodist bodies, were beginning to gain strength. Probably no more than 10 per cent of the population were actually members of Protestant churches in 1800. The churches were weak, both numerically and institutionally. Franklin H. Littell described the major preoccupation of the churches in those early days as ". . . the effort to win a people back to the churches they had frankly abandoned when support ceased to be compulsory, to Christianize and civilize an illiterate and semibarbarous people." [3]

This national missionary movement, lasting throughout most of the century and carrying the churches to the frontier settlements, imparted to American Christianity many of its characteristic qualities: revivalistic fervor and emotionalism, anti-intellectualism, practicality, democratic spirit. At the same time, those qualities came to permeate the society until it would not be a gross exaggeration to claim that Protestantism and Americanism were synonymous.

The latter part of the nineteenth century marks the second epoch in which Protestantism achieved a religious hegemony over American society. Though less than a majority of citizens were actual members of Protestant churches, it could be assumed that the average American would identify himself as a Protestant.[4] Protestantism, in turn, saw itself as the normative expression of American religion. It was this period of Protestant America that produced in the churches what Robert Handy has referred to as ". . . an entanglement and partial envelopment by an increasingly pluralistic and secularized culture." [5]

For even as the Protestant churches enjoyed their highest level of influence, forces had already been set in motion that would undermine their favored position in the culture. Modern thought was producing an increased amount of frank skepticism, anticlericalism, and even atheism. Immigration was bringing to America vast numbers of new citizens, mostly Roman Catholic with some Jews coming along later. Protestant America was becoming religiously pluralistic and predominantly secular.

The Protestant response to this third epoch has taken two main forms. On the one hand, a conservative Protestantism looked back with nostalgia to what is conceived of as the golden age of Protestant America. This point of view resists all attempts to modify the customs, manners, and morals of those days when Protestantism shaped the values of the society. Social change is, accordingly, a fall from grace.

A more liberal and enlightened viewpoint, on the other hand, sought to develop a valid Protestant social witness within the limits of the changed social situation. This viewpoint accepts secularization, pluralism, and the consequent loss of a favored position in American society.

The church's attitude toward nearly every major social issue has consequently undergone vast changes. Today, for example, Protestant churches advocate a form of family life based on mutuality and common consent. A century ago, they were defending a stern, authoritarian concept of the family on biblical grounds. Today most Protestant churches condone—and even encourage—family planning and yet it was a population largely Protestant of a previous era who enacted the Connecticut anti-birth-control laws which have only recently been declared unconstitutional.

These new attitudes have generally come in response to changed conditions in the social order or to new insights in the realm of ideas. On the whole, they were made belatedly, reluctantly, and often inadequately. Yet while some parts of the church have resisted change, other parts have rushed headlong into new situations, adopting new modes of thought too quickly and uncritically.

Though with the passage of time a new idea may win acceptance as part of the Christian consensus, seldom will it carry the day completely. More likely, the old ways of thinking will continue to coexist along with the new, after the heat of controversy has died down. Thus the bitter disputes over the historical criticism of the Bible have produced a modernist, critical school of biblical interpretation while biblical literalism continues to flourish in some quarters. The Protestant consensus is probably somewhere in between the two positions. This persistence of outmoded forms of thought helps to explain the bewildering diversity of contemporary Protestantism. The new idea, though it may replace the old one, seldom does away with it. The old idea continues its separate existence and retains the loyalty of its adherents.

The chapters following will discuss a number of specific issues about which the American churches have changed their minds and about which reasonable Christians continue to differ. It has not been possible to offer more than a brief survey of each topic. We will, nevertheless, try to evaluate the church's thought and activity in each of the selected areas. The writer has not hesitated, furthermore, to offer proposals for the church's actions in the future. While the reader may reject both the interpretations and the recommendations, the author hopes that any disagreement will lead those who dissent into further reading of their own.

1 THE EMERGENCE OF THE SECULAR STATE

ANY ATTEMPT to understand the place of the church in American society must first come to grips with the basic condition under which the church lives out its life in this country. That condition goes by several names: "the separation of church and state"; "the disestablishment of religion"; "the preservation of religious freedom." These phrases do not mean the same thing. In fact, it is often difficult to determine exactly what they do mean. This is one reason for the present-day controversy over the church-state relationship. Nearly everyone agrees that the separation of church and state is a Good Thing, but there is much less agreement on what the principle means or how it applies to specific issues.

All parties to the debate appeal to the authority of the founding fathers for clarification of the issue. That means they have to agree first as to just who the founding fathers were. Suppose we agree that the founding fathers were those who were instrumental in framing, adopting, and interpreting the Constitution in the late eighteenth century. That helps, but not very much. For as we look back on their words and deeds, it becomes clear that the founding fathers were not themselves all in agreement on the issue. The ambiguities of the church-state relationship have been in the American situation from the beginning. Our age is faced with the task of settling some of the fundamental issues which were allowed to remain unresolved by the founding fathers of the eighteenth century.

THE COLONIAL ERA

The causes for the traditional American concern for religious liberty are not hard to discover. It is a commonplace to say that many of the early settlers came to American shores to escape religious persecution in their native countries. The discovery that others—perhaps a majority—came simply to earn a better living does not invalidate the significance of religious freedom as a cause for immigration. Indeed, the colonies frequently advertised the fact of religious freedom as a way to attract settlers.

New England and Pennsylvania are the classic cases of colonial settlement for primarily religious reasons. It is significant that both Puritans and Quakers were fleeing from the hardships imposed upon them by the established Church of England. The Puritans opposed Episcopacy and the Book of Common Prayer but they were not opposed to the idea of establishment. They erected their own establishment in Massachusetts and Connecticut and it was much more authoritarian and doctrinaire than the Church of England had ever been. The religious freedom they sought was the freedom to establish a Puritan Commonwealth in which the "true order" of Christian life should be enshrined in the laws of the land.

The rigid rule of the Massachusetts Bay Colony soon provoked reactions. Before the colony had been in existence for a generation, Roger Williams made his famous flight to Providence where he established the first colony in which genuine religious freedom was maintained. His Rhode Island colony was considered something of a freak during colonial days, but it served as a haven for the persecuted of all colonies and it developed a tradition of religious toleration that was to become accepted by the new nation only after prolonged hesitation and controversy.

During the colonial period, another tendency in American religious life increased the antipathy of the colonists to the idea of an established church. This was the gradual but persistent spread of the Church of England establishment throughout the colonies. Virginia, Georgia, and the Carolinas had Anglican establishments from their earliest days. In Maryland, the original Roman Catholic settlers had made wide grants of religious liberty to all colonists but by 1688, when Maryland became a royal colony, Calvert's experiment in religious liberty had already been terminated and the Church of England became established there as well.

By the middle of the eighteenth century, Anglicans were living in all of the colonies, even in those of New England. Anglican parishes were established there under the protection of the royal governors but their work was carried on under strained circumstances. They had few members and very little money. Their clergy were mostly missionaries sent to the colonies by the English Society for the Propagation of the Gospel. Yet many leaders of the Church of England in America looked forward to the day when that church would enjoy the same rights of establishment in all the colonies as it enjoyed in England.

During this period, a plan was set in motion to bring a bishop to the colonies to supervise the work of the Anglican Church. With America's heritage of separation, it is difficult today to understand the political impact of this gesture. A bishop was more than just a presiding officer of the church who would confirm candidates, ordain clergy, and govern the ecclesiastical institution. In England, a bishop was an officer of the Crown and, frequently, a member of the House of Lords. He would outrank all the civil officials in the colonies, even the royal governors. His authority would extend throughout the whole of the British colonial seaboard. He would represent a danger to every non-Anglican religious body, for he might manage to set up a Church of England establishment over all the colonies. Moreover, he would represent a threat to colonial self-government for he could become the agency through which the will of king and Parliament might be imposed upon the unwilling colonists.

The colonists saw the danger and fought against it. New England Congregationalists accused their Anglican neighbors of plotting against their religious liberties, and the indications are that they were not far wrong. Anglicans in Virginia, where the church was already established, were not enthusiastic for a bishop. In the absence of higher authority, church affairs were left in the hands of the laity, and the Virginia gentlemen liked it that way. The clergy, who liked it less, appealed for a bishop but they had little power or influence.

The battle was fought out in England. The king was concerned to keep peace at home and the government was concerned to keep the support of the English dissenters. Therefore, the English friends of the New England Congregationalists got a better hearing in the councils of government than might otherwise have been expected. The maneuvering went on for some time with the result that no bishop was ever sent to the colonies. Nevertheless, the issue stirred up considerable feeling and, particularly in New England, it bred a deep-seated antagonism toward the British Crown and Parliament, a hostility that was to bear fruit later when the war for independence came.[1]

In those colonies in which the Church of England enjoyed the status of establishment, it managed to provoke the hostility of large segments of the society. In Virginia, for example, Anglicans represented only a small proportion of the population. Both Presbyterian and Baptist groups were growing rapidly. Yet the Church of England enjoyed exclusive official privileges and support. Until 1780, only Church of England clergy were permitted to officiate at marriages. When the local militia was activated, only Church of England clergy were recognized as chaplains.[2] Naturally, such measures aroused the resentment of other Christian bodies.

On the eve of the Revolution, the Church of England, secure and jealous of its prerogatives, was legally established from Maryland south to Georgia. At the same time, this church was weak both in membership and in local support. It was deeply resented by the numerous dissenters who made up a major portion of the population. In New England, the situation was different but the result was similar. Here the Anglican Church was only a tiny minority. Nonetheless, many of its clergy and laymen were busy fomenting plots to bring about the legal establishment of that church. In New England as in the South, the Church of England was hated and feared by its neighbors of various dissenting persuasions.

The religious life of America at the time of the Revolution, then, was marked by controversy, especially over the issue of religious freedom and the established church. Most Americans, when they thought at all about the established church, were against it. It is no wonder that, when the time came to form their own governments, the Americans made it their business to deal with the religious question in such a way that every American would henceforth be assured that his freedom to worship and to hold unpopular opinions would be respected by the laws of the new nation.

FROM REVOLUTION TO CONSTITUTION

While most of our attention in the present day is focused on the church-state issue in terms of the federal Constitution, it was on the state level that the battle for religious liberty was first fought and won. The debates on religious freedom produced some differences of opinion at the Constitutional Convention and afterward in the Congress that adopted the Bill of Rights. But the broad lines of toleration had already been laid down in the various states as they came together to adopt new constitutions beginning in the early years of the Revolution.

There were great variations in the official position toward religion in the new states. The Church of England had been established in the South, while the Congregational Church was established in New England. Rhode Island, by contrast, offered complete freedom to all sects and beliefs. In the short space of eleven years between independence and the opening of the Constitutional Convention, all of the Anglican establishments disappeared and the favored position of the Episcopal Church in New York vanished as well. South Carolina established "the Protestant Religion" in its Constitution of 1778 but this provision was soon abandoned. The Congregational establishments remained, but only in mild and truncated form, other sects being guaranteed equal treatment under the laws of the state. Some states retained religious tests for public office. Pennsylvania, for example, required of members of the State Assembly a statement of belief in the divine inspiration of both Old and New Testaments, though this provision was dropped in 1790. Delaware retained restrictions against Roman Catholics, but abolished them in 1792.[3]

By the time the Constitutional Convention met, established churches remained in only two states. Seven states still required some sort of religious test for public office, while four states had guaranteed complete religious freedom. Clearly, religious freedom represented the wave of the future and there was never a real chance that the new nation would permit any church to become legally established.

THE CONSTITUTION AND THE BILL OF RIGHTS

The question of religion barely intruded itself into the discussions and debates over the Constitution. It may be presumed that members of the Convention thought of religious liberty as belonging to the "reserved powers" of the states. Since state laws and practices differed, there was no clear course for the federal Constitution to follow. Nevertheless, one very important provision was adopted by the Convention. It remains today as part of Article VI of the Constitution: ". . . no religious test shall ever be required as a Qualification to any Office or public Trust under the United States."

The importance of this provision lies in the fact that it moved the new federal government ahead of most of the states in the area of religious freedom. The religious tests required in more than half the states at that time could well have provided the basis not for an established church, but for an informal establishment of Protestantism or Christianity or religion-in-general.

If we want clues as to the state of mind of the nation at large, we might inquire into the discussions that took place in the various states as they ratified the Constitution. Here there was considerable debate on the place of religion in the Constitution. As Canon Stokes has expressed it: "The state debaters were of three main groups: those who favored the clause in the Constitution . . . and thought it adequate; those who opposed this clause as superfluous, or dangerous to the cause of religion; and those who accepted it but wished it supplemented." [4]

The debates on the state level actually failed to settle the question. Those who believed that religion was in danger were not mollified by the course of events. They apparently represented the point of view that was expressed in the religious test provisions of some state constitutions. Most of the vocal religious elements favored the abandonment of religious tests, but asked for further guarantees for the freedom of religion. It was this issue, more than any other, that led five of the states to couple their ratification of the Constitution with appeals for the enactment of a Bill of Rights. When promises to this effect were made by George Washington and others, the anxiety over religious freedom died down.

Some conservative Protestants were afraid that the removal of religious tests would lead to all sorts of dangers in the future. Papists might seize control of the government—even infidels or Moslems. Their arguments were met, though probably their fears remained unallayed, by statements such as those of William Lancaster, of North Carolina:

> Let us remember that we form a government for millions not yet in existence. I have not the art of divination. In the course of four or five hundred years I do not know how it will work. This is most certain, that Papists may occupy that chair, and Mahometans may take it. I see nothing against it.[5]

Later generations have remarked on the absence in the Constitution of any reference to God. In contrast to the Declaration of Independence, the Constitution does not claim divine authority, nor does it rest its case for a national government on the divine will. It does not even make the customary (for the time) obeisance to the Almighty in its preamble.

This omission was duly noted and criticized at the time. The criticism stemmed from church groups, particularly the Presbyterians. They felt that, by failing to mention God in the Constitution, the Convention had left the country open to the possibility of a godless government. They voiced their fears in state legislatures and ratifying conventions as well as directly to Washington himself. His reply probably voiced the sentiments of the Convention. He pointed out to one such group of petitioners that "the path of true piety is so plain as to require but little political direction." The United States would not, therefore, seek to regulate religion, but would leave that sphere of life up to the clergy whose task it was to ensure its vitality.[6]

When the time came for the enactment of the Bill of Rights, the air had been somewhat cleared by the discussions over ratification. Freedom of religion obviously had to be included in the Bill of Rights. There remained conflicting views on the place that religion ought to occupy in the national life, but no group was strong enough to impose its view on the Congress. The result was a compromise in which all parties had to give a little. The principle of separation was established but the actual constitutional provision was intentionally ambiguous in order to cover disagreements which had to be smoothed over rather than finally settled.

RESULTS OF THE POLICY OF SEPARATION

The immediate results of the new constitutional provisions were not conspicuous. The Episcopal Church almost collapsed, to be sure, particularly in the South where it had previously enjoyed the benefits of tax revenues and the income from glebe lands. But this was a result of disestablishment on the state level. For the nation, the radical character of church-state separation was obscured for a time by the fairly homogeneous character of the American population and by the informal consensus that was to view America as a Protestant nation for more than a century.

Even though there was to be no established church in America, the informal Protestant establishment remained in fact. Invocations continued to be made at public functions. The courts still required oaths, though substitutions were permitted. Protestant religious teachings and forms of worship were used in the schools. Laws regulating Sabbath activities continued to be made and enforced. Other more subtle influences of Protestant ideas were accepted as the norm for the American nation.

This unofficial establishment of Protestantism went virtually unchallenged because most of America was still self-consciously Protestant. When the word "religion" was used, it normally meant Protestant Christianity, though often the user was unaware of this limitation. The few Catholics and Jews in America tended to go along with the Protestant consensus because they were included in it as variant strains of the normal religious expression.

There is much disagreement among the scholars as to just how Protestant the nation really was in the early days of its history. Few reliable figures are available before around 1820. Indications are that only a small percentage of the people were actually church members. Yet, even so, there was little vocal opposition to Protestant Christianity. The average man seems to have been indifferent to religion, though not antagonistic.

In contrast to the religious indifference of the general public, the formal corporate life of the nation accorded a high place to religion. Religious leaders were listened to with respect by the political leaders. In any community, the ministers stood out as important members of the society. In this context, it is only natural that the separation of church and state remained more a legal fiction than a reality.

Nevertheless, a revolutionary situation was in the making and time would reveal its extent and its significance. The United States of America had created the first genuinely secular state in modern history. It was a state in which the religious dimension of existence was given legal recognition but was left entirely on its own. It would receive neither regulation nor favor from the political community. It would be organized in any way it chose and would accept responsibility for its own institutional forms.

In practice, this came to mean that congregations could organize without the need to consult public officials. They raised their own funds and supported their own ministers and teachers. They spread their message by the power of persuasion, rather than by the coercive power of the state. Their success depended upon their own efforts. At the same time, the churches were free from state interference. The clergy were not required to act as official spokesmen or functionaries of the state. They were free to support the government or to criticize it as they saw fit. Thus the spheres of religion and politics were co-ordinate spheres and their relationship that of equals.

In the early years, these two notions of Protestant America and the secular state were held together without any sense of contradiction. It was only when immigration widened the meaning of religious pluralism in America that the inaccuracy of the term "Protestant America" began to be felt. In a sense, the history of religion in America can be seen as the working out of the dynamic of the secular state as it moved from Protestant America into the genuine religious pluralism that we know today. Many of the religious controversies in the political arena can best be understood against the background of this movement. There are still those who see America today as a Protestant nation and are willing to fight to keep it that way. Others admit the fact of religious pluralism, but insist that America is at least a basically religious nation which must prefer religion over atheism. There are still others who accept the logic of the secular state but wonder if a community can be genuinely neutral in religious matters without relegating God to the periphery of national life.

CONTEMPORARY ISSUES OF CHURCH-STATE RELATIONS

Later chapters will deal at some length with the implications of church-state separation for the American school, the college, and the political arena. Here the focus will be on those areas in which the relationship of the church and the state is a matter of serious controversy today. There are at least five aspects of this question which can be separated out for purposes of discussion. They include: (1) the continued legal enforcement of religious practices; (2) institutional co-operation between church and state; (3) issues involving the guarantee of religious freedom; (4) religious practices in public ceremonies; and (5) the place of morals and values in America's national life.

LEGAL ENACTMENT OF RELIGIOUS PRACTICES

This is an issue which has had considerable importance in the past but which is likely to assume less and less importance in the future. While there are still laws on the books which enforce the discipline of certain religious groups, nearly every religious body in the nation has disavowed them. Sabbath laws can still stir up controversy (see Chapter 2), but their complete disappearance is probably only a matter of time.

Most religious groups today would accept the principle that the Protestant has the right to observe the Sabbath because of his religious beliefs and the Roman Catholic has the right to avoid the use of contraceptives because of his religious beliefs, but neither may properly call upon the state to enforce this practice upon all its citizens. The corollary principle is that the state may be called upon to protect the right of the believer whenever it is challenged or denied. There may come a time, for example, when the state will have to prohibit an employer from dismissing an employee who, because he is a Christian, refuses to work on a Sunday. It may have to protect a Jewish employee who refuses to work on Yom Kippur.

The principle is clearer on paper than in practice. There is a vast, hazy area full of practices which are frowned upon by religious groups in the interest of public welfare and morals—an area in which the state does have the right to legislate. This area includes laws dealing with liquor, gambling, obscenity, and adultery. Roman Catholics for many years defended the anticontraceptive laws of Connecticut, not on the ground that contraception violates the discipline of the Roman Catholic Church but rather on the ground that contraception violates the natural law which is binding upon all men, whether they believe it or not.[7] Protestant opposition to gambling is based on similar reasoning.

Any law which regulates personal conduct ought to be based not on religious authority but on the common welfare of society. Churches cannot be allowed to dictate such laws, but must argue for or against them on the ground of their social consequences. Of course, different religious bodies hold different views as to what constitutes the common good of society. Indeed, different individuals hold different views of the common good whether they are church members or not. Where such different views are held, it is up to the legislators to balance off interest against interest and morality against morality. They may not be able to produce social harmony thereby, but at least they can help to prevent the dictation of legislation by religious groups.

INSTITUTIONAL CO-OPERATION OF CHURCH AND STATE

The issue of co-operation between government and the churches is very complicated and likely to become even more so in the future. It is this co-operation that advocates of church-state separation have in mind when they refer to the "wall of separation" that must exist between the church and the state. The actual state of affairs shows the inadequacy of this conception.

It might be pointed out in passing that the "wall of separation" is not a legally binding conception, nor is it an explanation of the meaning of the First Amendment to the Constitution. It is merely a phrase used by Thomas Jefferson in expressing his own view of the Constitution. Jefferson was not a member of the Constitutional Convention, nor of the Congress that enacted the Bill of Rights, so it is difficult to see how his "wall of separation" phrase can be invoked as the authoritative statement of constitutional relationship of church and state.

The experience of schools and colleges shows how difficult it is to maintain any wall of separation in practice. The "G. I. Bill of Rights," for example, provided funds for World War II veterans to attend college. These funds were understood to be a benefit to the veteran, not to the college although, of course, the college benefited too. Consistent enforcement of the wall-of-separation doctrine would have denied veterans the right to use these public funds to attend church colleges. The result would have been a restriction of the freedom of the veteran and a form of discrimination against the church-sponsored college.

Similarly, public health programs customarily make use of the schools as a convenient medium for reaching all the children of a community. Medical and dental examinations are conducted on school grounds and children are excused from classes for their examinations. Such programs normally extend to parochial schools because they are concerned with the health of the students and not with education. Yet the administration of the program requires public officials to co-operate with parochial school officials and once again the wall of separation becomes impossible to maintain.

As the federal government enters into the field of welfare at the local level, it is becoming committed more and more to the view that it should co-operate with local government and citizens' groups in co-ordinated attacks upon specific problems such as poverty. Since churches are traditionally active in this field, maintaining hospitals, homes, counseling services, charity programs, and the like, it seems clear that churches and government will have to learn to co-operate if they are not to stand hopelessly in each other's way. As time goes on, we can expect to see the distinctions breaking down between "public welfare" and "private charity." This will require a serious rethinking of the cliché about the mythical "wall of separation."

This rethinking may well take the form of working out a theoretical distinction between the church's primary role—the maintenance and propagation of its religious beliefs and practices —and its co-operative role as a social agency. Both functions are necessary for the full life of the church, but the second function can be recognized and shared by the state in a way that the first function cannot be. The distinction is admittedly fuzzy in practice. Church-state co-operation can be entered into only in limited ways and with great caution. Both parties have to keep their eyes open to the very real dangers which are inevitably involved in such a sensitive and controversial area.

ISSUES INVOLVING RELIGIOUS FREEDOM

The constitutional guarantee of religious freedom causes some difficulty because it accords to religion a favored place in society held by no other aspect of life and thought. Because of their religious beliefs, certain citizens may have to be allowed to do certain things which other citizens are not allowed to do. Thus the courts have upheld the right of Jehovah's Witnesses to refuse to salute the flag. They have recognized the right of religious pacifists to refuse military service, while the status of those who object to military service on political or philosophical grounds is still cloudy.

The reason for this apparent contradiction goes back to the framing of the Constitution. Religious persecution was never far from the minds of the founding fathers, whether they were Christians or skeptics. The only cure for persecution, they recognized, was freedom of religion. The disestablishment of the church meant the church's freedom from state control. The freedom of the church does not exist because the state in its beneficence grants to the church a freedom it could just as easily retract. Rather, freedom of religion exists in America because of the conviction of the founders that religion is an area of life into which the political authorities have no right to intrude. The religious institution is free from state control.

It is this immunity from state control that has resulted in the practice of exempting churches from the payment of taxes. This issue is worth further discussion because it is likely to become the subject of bitter controversy in the near future. Unfortunately, most of the discussion of the tax-exemption problem to date has been based on irrelevant considerations.

Many responsible voices have already been raised to protest against tax exemptions for churches on the ground that tax exemptions constitute a subsidy for religion and are therefore unconstitutional. Others attempt to justify the exemptions on the ground that churches perform socially useful functions which the state may encourage with tax exemptions in the same way that it has encouraged nonprofit schools, hospitals, and charitable foundations.

The matter appears in quite a different light when the tax exemption is seen not as a subsidy but as a recognition by government of the limits of its authority. The government simply does not have the right to tax the church. The taxing power implies a predominance of the government over the person or organization taxed. The Constitution denies that the government has power over the churches. It rejects the absolutist claim that the state has unlimited rights within its borders. In America, churches exist by right, not by the suffrance of the government. If the government's right to tax the church were admitted, then the door would be open to the possibility of harassment and eventual annihilation of the religious institution.

This view vindicates the freedom of the churches from taxation, but only within narrow limits. The Constitution guarantees the free exercise of religion, which implies that the functions of worship, teaching, and welfare work are justifiably exempted from taxation. But most churches today possess more property than that which they use for these essential functions. They own houses for their clergy. They own buildings which they hold for profit. They own businesses which they operate for profit. There is no justification for exemption of these properties from taxation. In fact, many municipalities have already begun to tax such properties at regular rates.

There is no doubt that some churches have abused their tax-free status by acquiring income-producing properties and taking them off the tax rolls. The result has been not only a loss of tax revenue, but an undue concentration of economic wealth and power in the hands of the ecclesiastical institution. The next few years will probably see many attacks on the tax-exempt status of the churches. The outcome will depend largely upon how the churches meet the attack. If they accept the taxation of their income-bearing property and the exemption of their worship, teaching, and welfare facilities, then the changes can be brought about easily and the financial losses, though great, will be bearable. But if the churches fight any thought of change, then the resulting battle will produce bitterness and hostility that will do immeasurable damage to the whole church far into the future.

The status of military chaplains also poses difficult problems for the maintenance of church-state separation and religious freedom. The First Amendment would seem to require the government to permit soldiers and sailors access to worship and spiritual direction while on duty. This requirement implies the existence of a corps of chaplains who can be housed, supported, and transported with the troops. It involves the incorporation of the chaplaincy into the whole scheme of military discipline. It also places the government in the embarrassing position of having to establish criteria for recognizing ordination or refusing to recognize it.

The courts would probably have no trouble in seeing the logic of this arrangement, were the subject to be raised. True, it does place government and churches in intimate relationships, but such intimacy seems unavoidable under the circumstances. What is more likely to come under attack is the use of government funds to support the chaplaincy program. While the Constitution does not forbid the government to provide access to chaplains and church services, it would seem to require the churches themselves to provide the chaplains and to support their work financially.

Sooner or later, the military chaplaincy will be challenged in the courts. It seems clear that, should this happen, the courts will have to decide that government funds cannot be used to pay chaplains. The result will be that the churches will have to take over their support. The expense might be considerable, but there is no reason why the churches cannot meet it. And while the financial hardship might be great, the churches might achieve a certain moral stature by resourcefully meeting this new responsibility.

RELIGION IN PUBLIC CEREMONIES

The ceremonial use of religion at public functions raises questions, but less serious ones. Few people would claim that they are damaged when they are subjected to a prayer or a blessing that contains doctrine to which they do not subscribe. Yet there is an issue involved, one that is theological rather than constitutional.

The prayer at the public meeting is a holdover from the era of Christendom. Christendom saw the church and the state as two aspects of a single society. The church, in short, was the nation on its knees. Aside from commitment to the separation of church and state, Americans can no longer subscribe to a doctrine that "Christens" an entire community. Corporate prayer is the prayer of a company of believers. Corporate prayer in a public gathering made up indiscriminately of believers and non-believers is at best a meaningless form and at worst a travesty on the meaning of prayer. It offends the sensibilities of the non-believer and compromises the integrity of the religious community.

In spite of this stern view of the matter, the practice undoubtedly will continue indefinitely. It may inconvenience a few individuals, but small inconveniences seldom stir people up much. Then too, it is hard for anyone to oppose prayer on whatever grounds; Americans do not take kindly to those who come out publicly against God. If any progress is to be made in this direction, it will have to come from the church leaders themselves. They will have to point out the contradictions involved in offering prayers to God on behalf of assembled multitudes who do not believe in him. Only as the churches themselves call a halt to this debatable practice is it likely to disappear.

VALUES IN AMERICAN LIFE

The agonizing question of the place of morals, ethics, and values in the public life of a secular state has been with Americans from the beginning. It was posed at the time of the ratification of the Constitution, by men who feared that without an establishment of religion, America would become a godless nation. In one sense, of course, they were right. A secular state is officially godless, not that it repudiates religious faith but in that it cannot acknowledge the validity of any religion or even of religion itself.

The concern of those men of the eighteenth century was different from our concern today. They were convinced that religion offered the only basis for morality, public or private. If one denies God, then all the rules disappear and the result is anarchy. This view was held by skeptics as well as Christians. Benjamin Franklin accepted this argument for religion, though he himself was not a practicing Christian.

That argument is meaningless for our time, for we no longer believe that one must be religious in order to be moral. The exemplary lives of numerous atheists and agnostics negate such a belief. Our question is more difficult. We have accepted the disestablishment of the church and the accompanying view that the church's teaching office is restricted to her own members. Religious and moral training is a function of the church only insofar as it concerns those within the fold. Yet church membership amounts to less than half of the population. Who is to teach the rest? How are the values of a democratic society to be inculcated? By what authority are they to be taught?

One obvious answer is that the public schools must teach values. Yet is there not a danger that if the schools teach values, they will become something of a new state church?

Will Herberg has suggested that the real religion of America is something called "the American way of life." [8] In this context, religious beliefs become mere personal aberrations which are not to be taken too seriously provided they do not affect the citizen's basic loyalty to the state and the values of society. It is arguable that the democratic faith has already become a religion and that the schools which teach this religion constitute an established church because they unite the teaching of values with the coercive power of the state.[9]

If this is so, then Christians of America are indeed caught on the horns of a dilemma. Protestants, Catholics, and Jews in America share in a general acceptance of democracy and the values it entails. Yet, according to their religious views, these are agreements about secondary matters, for the social and political realm is secondary to the level on which man owes primary allegiance to God. But on that primary level fundamental disagreements occur. Our very existence as separate religious groups testifies to the depth and the scope of these disagreements. Our disagreements with skeptics and atheists go even deeper.

Because we coexist peaceably in a free society, we are constantly led to stress our agreements for the sake of social harmony. Thus our agreements, though secondary, are brought into the foreground while our disagreements, which are fundamental, recede into the background and are consequently downgraded. The disagreements are relegated to the category of "private opinions," which have little significance. "It doesn't make any difference what you believe so long as you lead a good life" is the logical outcome of this unnatural situation. We beg the larger questions because they arouse antagonism. The result may be social and political consensus, but it means sure death for Christian faith and any other religious faith as well.

Should the teaching of values be left to the schools? Is this not permitting the schools to teach a religion—a highly suspect variety of religion? Does it not open the door to the political manipulation of values and attitudes that the state ought have no right to touch? If the schools do not teach morals and values,

who will? How about that half of the population that is not related to any church? Must we condone the increasing anarchy in
the realm of values in our society?

These questions are easier to raise than to answer. The difficulty is that they are so seldom raised. Our generation will have
to take this whole problem far more seriously than it has up to
now. Somehow we must find ways of establishing the priority of
that which is primary, without losing the wide agreement which
we now have in the area that is secondary. Perhaps this process
will require all of us, whatever our religious convictions, to raise
the more significant question: Is our religious faith meaningful if
it does not produce some change in our attitudes and our actions
in the social and political area? This is an old and perplexing
question, but it demands an answer.

2 POLITICS—AFTER THE GREAT CRUSADE

THE RELATIONSHIP of religion and politics has always been a troublesome problem in American life. The difficulty may be seen as an outgrowth of the doctrine of separation of church and state. Or, on the other hand, the strategy of separation may itself be seen as merely one way of dealing with a perennial problem. The issue is often posed in the form of a statement such as, "Religion is a private affair" or, "You shouldn't mix religion and politics."

Statements like these are usually heard when some clergyman makes reference in a sermon to political events, or when a church body takes a specific stand on some controversial issue. The cynic might observe that the protest is made only when the protester disagrees with the stand taken. In any case, a sermon or a church pronouncement on a controversial issue is very likely to draw the fire of opponents on these grounds: religion and politics do not mix; religion is a private affair.

The theologian would naturally respond that this kind of criticism is based on a faulty understanding of the way in which God works in the affairs of men. It seems to presume that life can be divided into neat compartments labeled "Politics," "Art," "Economics," "Family Life," and so on, until we finally come to the Sunday morning compartment labeled "Religion." But Christians can recognize no such artificial division of life. God rules over all of life and if the Christian faith has any meaning at all, it must necessarily have meaning in the political realm as well as in private life.

The theologian is right, of course, but having rejected the compartment theory of life, he has still not solved any problems. When we examine the religion-and-politics question from the perspective of history, we can see some point to the criticism. Actually, the view that "religion is a private affair" grows out of America's tradition of religious liberty, and a good deal may be said for it.

Perhaps the significance of the "private affair" approach can best be seen when it is contrasted with its opposite. In colonial days, Massachusetts was a model ecclesiastical commonwealth. Religion was not only established by law, but the community was founded on the conviction that religion was a public matter. The political institution was required to safeguard Christian morals. The state was under the obligation to do the will of God. The church was to provide the teaching that would enable the public official to see his duty. The "Platform of Church Discipline" made this duty specific:

It is the duty of the magistrate to take care of matters of religion. . . . The end of the magistrate's office is not only the quiet and peaceable life of the subject in matters of righteousness and honesty, but also in matters of godliness.[1]

The arrangement was tidy. The civil authorities would direct the religious life of the people, while the ministers directed the magistrates. This was no mere theory to be stated and then ignored. There were adequate instruments to make the notion function. Any candidate who was unable to secure the endorsement of the ministers was unlikely to be elected.

One of the more interesting customs of the period was the election sermon, which was preached at the installation of public officials. In this sermon, the minister would set forth the task of the civil authorities in upholding the course of true religion. He would customarily lay the theological foundation for the Puritan Commonwealth, referring to heroic past and contrasting the piety and true godliness of the founding fathers with the moral decline of the present age. If all this seems somewhat familiar, it may merely demonstrate that Americans haven't moved as far from their Puritan heritage as they seem to think.

Colonial Massachusetts offers a good illustration of a society which believes that the state has the duty to further specifically religious ends. In such a society, religion is a public matter. Its public character is manifested in the tendency of the clergyman to tell the statesman how things ought to be run and to tell the electorate who ought to run them. In this perspective, we can describe the history of American politics as a process of secularization in which the political realm has gradually freed itself from its close ties with the religious establishment. The separation of church and state was part of this larger movement. Separation meant that thenceforth a man's religious beliefs and practices were to be his own affair. Conversely, the state was to be free to pursue its essentially political ends, unhampered by the need to maintain the sanctions of true religion.

To the Christian, secularization may seem to be a major blow to Christian faith and life. It implies a godless and amoral state. Yet, as we have seen, this has not been the result in America. Certainly it is no longer necessary in politics to justify every course of action by resting the case on Holy Scripture. Religious sanctions are no longer regarded as an adequate basis for public morality. But this does not mean that there is, therefore, no public morality. On the contrary, public morality still exists, but it must appeal to a broad conception of the common good, rather than to the religious beliefs of its supporters.

The case for the independence of politics from religion was stated best, perhaps, by John F. Kennedy, during his presidential campaign of 1960. A number of Protestant churchmen voiced the suspicion that, because he was a Roman Catholic, Kennedy might not be faithful to the tradition of church-state separation which Americans have come to regard as normative. Sensing the damage that this suspicion was doing to his campaign, Kennedy chose to deal openly with the subject at a meeting with the Greater Houston Ministerial Association early in September. Among his other remarks, he said:

> I believe in an America where the separation of Church and State is absolute—where no Catholic prelate would tell the President (should he be a Catholic) how to act and no Protestant minister would tell his parishioners for whom to vote. . . .
> I believe in a President whose views on religion are his own private affair, neither imposed upon him by the nation or imposed by the nation upon him as a condition to holding that office. . . . Contrary to common newspaper usage, I am not the Catholic candidate for President. I am the Democratic Party's candidate for President, who happens also to be a Catholic. . . . I do not speak for my church on public matters—and the church does not speak for me.[2]

Kennedy saw "religion is a private affair" to mean that his religious convictions were strictly his own business and not public property. He did not contend that his convictions would make no impression upon his conduct of public office—indeed, he went so far as to say that if he were ever called on to make a decision as President that his conscience would not permit, then he would resign the office. But he did state clearly that he would not accept political direction from any ecclesiastical official.

This is the legitimate meaning of the aphorism, "You can't mix religion and politics." The protest is not against religion as a set of convictions, held with fervor and dedication, making their force felt in every decision. The proper objection is, rather, to the intrusion into political life of an officious ecclesiasticism which makes demands that lie outside its proper province. The rejection of ecclesiastical direction of political affairs is a sound and valid product of the American experience.

As we look at the relationship of religion and politics in American history, it is possible to discern a three-step progression in the nature of that relationship. In its earliest form, it was characterized chiefly by the use of political power to maintain Protestant practices and to safeguard institutional interests. Then there came a period in which Protestant groups worked in politics for humanitarian causes, usually in conjunction with similar non-Protestant groups. Still more recently, there has appeared a tendency to analyze and evaluate political issues in theological categories beyond the level of ideology and moralism.

THE PROTECTION OF PROTESTANT INTERESTS

The most obvious way in which American Protestantism has made itself felt in political life has been in the espousal of legislation to enforce morality which has no other sanction than the support of the Protestant churches. Murder is forbidden by the churches, but it is also forbidden by the canons of sound community life, so the prohibition of murder does not fall into this category. The Protestant heritage has, however, produced laws that outlaw gambling, obscenity, indecent dress, and vagrancy. The long crusade for the prohibition of alcoholic beverages is another example of Protestant morality enforced by law. The notorious Sunday "blue laws" are perhaps the most enduring legislation of this character.

Protestant political activity of this sort is a vestige of the days of the established churches, which viewed themselves as the appointed keepers of the public morals. After the churches were legally disestablished, the Protestant community as a whole functioned to ensure that Protestant moral standards were enacted into laws which were binding upon all citizens, Protestant or otherwise. Without ever formulating any theories about the matter, the church leaders encouraged the enactment of legislation which would make America safe for Protestantism.

The most prominent of these laws were those relating to the Sabbath. These so-called "blue laws" are based on the conviction that God intended the Sabbath for a day of rest and that the laws ought to protect this rest. The laws are Christian in character because Sunday is the day chosen, a fact which confounds and confuses both Jews and Seventh-day Adventists. They are Protestant in character because Roman Catholicism has not traditionally frowned upon either commerce or recreation on the Lord's Day.

Sabbath legislation came under attack as long ago as Andrew Jackson's administration, when there was a spirited campaign to permit the delivery of mail on Sunday. The fight was long and bitter. It was spearheaded by Jacksonian Democrats and opposed by a coalition which can best be described as a "Protestant establishment." Jackson was treated rather viciously by the Protestant clergy who called him "atheist" and "antichrist" although he was a faithful Presbyterian. The Sunday mail proposal was defeated, but the chief result of the conflict was a residue of bitter anticlericalism in Jacksonian democracy.

If Sabbatarian legislation ever had any justification, it was soon outmoded, for the character of the American population changed. As the number of Catholic immigrants who had quite a different attitude toward the Sabbath swelled, Protestants fought harder to maintain the old ways. For them, Sunday sports and entertainment were not merely un-Protestant. They were unchristian and un-American. Protestants viewed the increasing Roman Catholic immigration with considerable uneasiness because it contributed to what they saw as the decline of traditional moral standards. They saw in Sabbath legislation one way to prevent change from occurring.

But the changes did occur. As time went on, Sunday observances became less restrictive. Many of the old laws disappeared, while others were unenforced. Sunday movies, dancing, sports and theatrical performances have normally been approved when submitted to popular referendum, even in predominantly Protestant areas.

Yet today, when the idea of a legally enforced Sabbath rest is a total anachronism, efforts are still made by Protestant churchmen to reinvigorate the old Sabbath customs. Within the past few years, the issue of Sunday sales by retail stores has been revived under a curious set of circumstances.

The growth of suburbs has created a greater reliance on the automobile for shopping. It is often more convenient for a family to shop on weekends when father is at home and the car is available. At the same time, there has been an increase in the number of working wives who have very little time for shopping, car or no car. The result has been a heavy pressure for shopping facilities which are open at night and on weekends. Businessmen have naturally been quick to meet the needs of consumers and shopping centers have sprung up in suburban areas. These facilities normally keep hours that the traditional city businessman would regard as unbearable. Moreover, the new shopping centers compete with downtown merchants, especially department stores, and these older retail outlets are beginning to feel the pinch of competition.

Although many states and municipalities have laws prohibiting or greatly restricting retail sales on Sunday, the new suburban retailers have frequently ignored the laws because they have been for so long unenforced. Sometimes the merchants have contested the laws in the courts and other times they have tried to have the laws changed or repealed. But at this point, there has occurred one of those strange phenomena that result when ecclesiastical interests intersect with economic interests and the issue is fought out in political terms.

All over the country, church groups have rushed in to defend the prohibition of Sunday retail sales. Nowadays, they usually make some attempt to gain support on other grounds than merely that of the Protestant doctrine of the Sabbath. The laws are on the books and they ought to be enforced; otherwise, respect for the law will suffer. A man ought to have a day off from work so that he can relax with his family. Sunday is such a day. It is not a religious holiday, but an opportunity for rest and family activity.

The economic interest enters when religious groups begin to realize how their interests coincide with those of the merchants who keep conventional store hours. Those merchants are willing to pay the cost of the political campaign to keep Sunday for God and the alliance of religious interest with economic interest is cemented—with money.

The churches are interested in making it easier to be Christian. Churchgoing is easier when there is nothing else to do on Sunday anyway. The churches are frequently unwilling to face the competition of shopping in addition to that of golf, swimming, week-end trips, and work on the front lawn. When this happens, the churches find themselves engaged in politics, not to raise the level of political life, not to help build a better community, but to protect the organizational interests of the churches themselves. In many parts of the country, Roman Catholic leaders have joined their Protestant counterparts in protesting Sunday retail sales. The Catholic view of the Sabbath is quite different from that of Protestantism, but the organizational interests of the two groups are identical. Thus, although Sabbath legislation is clearly obsolescent, the peculiar conjunction of religious pressure and economic interest makes it practically impossible to abolish.

Protestant organizational interests have similarly been involved in Protestant protests against the President's decision to send a diplomatic envoy to the Vatican. There is apparently no doubt as to the President's authority to make such an appointment if he deems it in the national interest. Yet when President Franklin D. Roosevelt made such an appointment, he was severely criticized in Protestant circles. When President Harry Truman contemplated a similar appointment, he was so savagely attacked by Protestants that he dropped the plan.

In neither case was there any question about the morality or the rectitude of the appointment. Protestants called it a violation of the constitutional separation of church and state. Yet the case was tried not in the courts but in the pulpits and the religious press. The amount of invective, distortion, and personal attack in the controversy did little to raise the standards of American political behavior. Indeed, that was not the concern of the Protestant opposition. The Protestant leaders saw the appointment as a gain in prestige for Roman Catholicism and a corresponding setback for Protestantism. Their ends were institutional, not theological.

PROTESTANTISM AND HUMANITARIAN CAUSES

This survey of Protestant political activity may seem rather grim, but it does not tell the whole story. Along with an unfortunate preoccupation with narrow institutional concerns, American Protestantism has displayed a broad humanitarian concern that has provided a creative leaven in American political life.

There have always been active reform movements in America. The objects of their concern have been many and various. As old battles have been won, new antagonists have continually appeared. Shortly after the Revolution, the Pennsylvania Quakers led a movement to reform the prison system, substituting rehabilitation for vengeance and alleviating the hard lot of the prisoner. This same period saw the beginning of the movement for bettering the lot of women. Antislavery movements were also beginning at the end of the eighteenth century.

Charity has always been a major Christian concern and this has been especially true of American Protestantism. Throughout the years, charity has taken many forms. Only in recent years has this concern for the poor moved directly into the area of politics as the complexity and institutionalization of industrial civilization has made private charity inadequate. The Protestant concern for education has been such an important part of the church's life in America that it will be taken up in separate chapters.

All of these movements have been inspired by the same Christian concern for a better life for all men. Because they have been directed at broad humanitarian causes, they have been able to enlist the co-operation of non-Protestant groups, thereby increasing their impact on the total society. It is this ability of diverse groups to co-operate in achieving political ends that has provided much of the progressive ferment in American politics and it can best be understood in the context of American political life.

Americans are so accustomed to their peculiar political environment that they normally fail to appreciate its uniqueness. The salient fact of American politics is that it is a politics of coalition. America may not have a multiparty system, but the parties that she does have are massive and often hardly coherent coalitions of special interests and competing groups. The parties themselves exist to seize and hold public office. They maintain no consistent ideological basis, a fact that is bewildering to the foreigner and often infuriating to Americans themselves.

When any great end is to be achieved in America, it is not usually accomplished through the formation of a new political party or an organization that can arouse mass support. It is done, rather, by the dedicated work of small, interested groups working within the established parties. Occasionally, they may win their way by actually capturing one of the major parties. More often, they demonstrate sufficient popular strength to make it worthwhile for one of the major parties to include their goal as an integral part of the party program.

At the turn of the century, the Progressive movement effectively captured the Republican party for a time, but progressives later found it just as easy to do business with the Democrats who soon discovered the potency of the reform issue. Later the labor movement won its way in the Democratic party through the New Deal, but it now enjoys significant support in both major parties. More recently, the civil rights movement won the respectful attention of both parties before it was possible to enact the Civil Rights Act of 1964.

With respect to the churches, this aspect of American political life has had a particular importance. There has never been a "Christian party" in America, although there have occasionally been ill-fated attempts to form one. We take this fact for granted, of course, but it is most significant for the quality and shape of our politics. Germany, France, Spain, and Italy have all had

Christian parties of some sort within the past generation and some of them enjoy power today. It has been to America's great fortune that she has had no such thing.

America has, instead, the politics of coalition, a kind of politics that requires its own peculiar strategy and produces its own kind of results. Christians ought to understand its peculiarities if they are to make any sense out of their own political environment and the relationship of religion to that brand of politics. In the first place, it helps to explain why so many Christians can express impatience at the church's relative impotence in the political realm. "Why doesn't the church *do* something about . . . ?" (civil rights, the atomic bomb, capital punishment, crime in the cities— you name it). The question assumes that the ecclesiastical institution ought to be directing the course of American political life. This point of view assigns a primacy to the religious organization that is foreign to the American experience. Even the Roman Catholic Church was able to exert this kind of leadership only in the very early days, when most of her members were unlettered immigrants who desperately needed an authority to help them become oriented to the new and strange society in which they found themselves.

The most the churches have been able to do has been to point to the moral implications of a political issue. The advancement of the cause has typically been the work of groups of church members acting in their capacity as citizens, in conjunction with Christians of other persuasions as well as with Jews, Unitarians, secularists, and whoever else is able to feel the same concern for the issue. More often than not, a secular group has led the way, as in the fight for the abolition of slavery and, more recently, the struggle for civil rights for Negroes. The National Association for the Advancement of Colored People and the American Civil Liberties Union are examples of such trail-blazing secular organizations.

But to say that these organizations are secular in character is not to demean or disown them. Most of them contain numbers of committed Christians who have seen their role to be that of working out their convictions in political terms. Franklin D. Roosevelt stood in this tradition of Christian secularism. When asked for his political ideology, he replied, "I am a Christian and a Democrat." The answer was not so naïve as it has sometimes been made to appear.

Churchmen often regard secular organizations for human betterment as a judgment upon the church. If the church were really doing its job, we wouldn't need NAACP, ACLU, SANE, World Affairs Council, and all the rest. But this is a mistaken conception of the role of the church. Any issue that commands broad support on the basis of the common good of society is likely to be better served by a secular organization than by one under church sponsorship. Christians do well to support such organizations with both their money and their efforts.

This does not mean that church groups have no place in political life, but it does say something about the nature of their place. It means that a group of churchmen who have strong convictions about pacifism or race relations or birth control may come together as a group within the larger body of their church. They will be set apart on the basis of their common convictions and they will act, in a sense, on behalf of the whole church. Yet they need not set themselves against their church if they can recognize the right of their fellow churchmen to disagree with them or even to oppose their efforts. They need not claim moral superiority for their view, nor insist that the whole church adopt it. The time may come when they will carry their whole church with them, but if that never happens, it still does not mean either that they were wrong to try to work out their convictions, or that the church body is necessarily the agent of the Evil One.

To carry the process further, our "sect" of enthusiasts who feel themselves called in a special way to a political vocation, may, as a church group, restrict their numbers to fellow church members. But whether they do or not, they will find it expedient to co-operate with other, nonchurch groups for the achievement of their ends. They will have to learn to work through the major parties. They will have to discover ways of bringing pressure on those in power. They will have to employ the many strategies and tactics that have become traditional for groups working for political ends in the United States. They will learn the uses and abuses of power and they will learn to compromise with evil. All of this is part of the American political process. The important lesson is that in politics, Christians have to act in harmony with others who share their political convictions but who may differ, perhaps radically, on the values that underlie those convictions.

The liberal or progressive strand in American politics has been our most sensitive and creative tradition, and from the earliest days it has had a considerable amount of Christian influence. In the early years, that influence was largely Protestant but the Protestant impact has weakened in this century. The reason has not been so much a decline of Protestant progressivism or political responsibility. It has been, rather, the sheer weight of numbers. There are simply more Jews and Roman Catholics now active in liberal politics. Perhaps this is because Jews and Catholics, being less rooted in the ideology of the American past, are more open to the possibility of social change. Or perhaps it is because their religious tradition gives both Catholics and Jews a greater sense of the reality of community and a corresponding motivation to work out their religious commitment in political terms. Whatever the cause, there is little doubt that Protestant leadership of political liberal movements has, in recent years, taken a back seat.

This is not to say that Protestants are no longer active in such movements. They are still active and their influence is not negligible. Of course, it must be conceded that many Protestants who get caught up in liberal political causes become discouraged with the prevailing conservatism of the religious institution and, as a result, frequently give up all identification with their church. Nevertheless, it would be a mistake to conclude that, because most political action is undertaken by secular groups, religion is no longer an important or creative factor in American politics.

BEYOND IDEOLOGY: RECOGNIZING THE ACTUALITIES
OF POLITICS

The preceding paragraphs would seem to indicate that Christian participation in politics is to be identified with the furthering of certain specific causes. Indeed, this is the substance of most approaches to the subject of the Christian in politics. The Christian is supposed to serve only good causes, most of which are predictable: clean and honest government, efficient law enforcement, social welfare, peace, etc. He is to think independently and not subject himself to the rule of a party. He is to keep his integrity by refraining from engaging in shady deals. He is to raise the level of politics by being honest, idealistic, upright and just. And, of course, he is to seek out and espouse the Christian position on every issue.

Yet any reading of American political history finds Protestants on every side of every issue. The participation of Protestants on both sides of the Civil War has frequently been cited. The Episcopal Church, which this writer knows best, seems to contain both the most conservative and the most radical members of any community. In Protestantism as a whole, the rule holds good that if any church makes a pronouncement on any controversial issue, part of that same church is sure to denounce it. The resulting situation scandalizes conscientious churchmen and absolutely bewilders the secular world outside the church.

Any number of reasons have been suggested as to why this should be true. One reason, certainly, is a breakdown in church discipline. Perhaps our witness in the public arena is weak because our convictions are weak and our ecclesiastical loyalties are weak. To be sure, this is a contributing factor. But even if church discipline were strong and vital, it would provide no total solution to the problem of political pluralism. It is by no means clear that in a political controversy, all of the true, committed, and disciplined Christians are to be found on the same side.

Of course there is the easy explanation that Christians merely use their religion as a cloak for their economic and class interests. This Marxian analysis of religion has enough truth in it to require that it be taken seriously. Certainly there are those who look to the church to justify their interests, habits, and prejudices. More subtly, there is an inevitable tendency for religious people to try to make sense theologically out of the concrete conditions of their lives. Their natural impulse is to explain, and incidently to justify, the existing order of things, rather than to undercut the only kind of life they know. Thus, a successful businessman will be likely to find moral sanctions for the notion of getting ahead, while a teacher will find ways to uphold the spiritual values of education. In this sense, religion does tend to serve and buttress class and economic interests.

In recent years, however, more thoughtful theologians have begun to face the shattering conclusion that sincere and informed Christians can honestly analyze political issues and find themselves on opposite sides of the fence. Their differences may be minor. They may agree on the ends to be attained but disagree on the particular measure in dispute. Or the differences may be major, involving such a difference of outlook as to make it impossible for either to see any validity in the view of the other. Their differences may be rooted in their education, their upbringing, or their nontheological commitments. They may represent conscious choices or quite unconscious personality traits. They may be obvious or they may completely defy analysis.

To take just one significant ideological difference which can obscure the similarity of religious convictions, consider the traditional liberal-conservative dichotomy which may be rooted in personality structure as well as in intellectual commitments. Politically speaking, there is a liberal way of being a Christian and there is a conservative way. Each of them has validity as well as limitations.

The liberal's views on politics are imbued with a passion for justice and mercy for all men. He is concerned to use the political processes in order to help people to better lives. He sees potentialities for better life in the present affluence, in the uses of technology, and in the spread of knowledge. He believes that Americans have the power to reshape society and make it serve the highest ends of man. He believes that the purpose of politics should be to put all of our resources to work for the good of all.

As he looks about him, however, the liberal sees poverty and squalor in the midst of plenty. In a democratic society, he sees lingering signs of inequality, often enforced by law. He sees evils that seem remediable and he believes that Christians ought to work for social changes that will eliminate these evils. The liberal has a deep confidence in man's capacity for good and he believes that people ought to make better use of it. Perfection may not be attainable, but improvement is possible.

The conservative, on the other hand, is less convinced about the possibilities for change. He knows that change is not necessarily good of itself. He knows that civilization is only a thin shell over the forces of chaos and that every change, good or bad, opens up another crack in that shell. He prefers an orderly society and knows that change is a constant threat to order. Change may solve a small problem while it brings with it a greater and unanticipated evil. The future must grow out of the past, so the past must be treated with reverence. Society is an organic growth, not a mechanism. It is like a tree: if you chop down the tree today because you need the space, you may decide tomorrow that you miss the shade, but then it is too late to bring back the tree.

If the liberal has convictions about man's capacity for good, the conservative is more impressed by his capacity for evil. Change does not eliminate evil; it merely provides it with a new environment and new opportunities. If the conservative does not fear the future, he is at least skeptical about its possibilities. If he does not believe he can keep change from occurring, he sees his role as that of slowing down change, moderating the excessive enthusiasm of the militant progressive, making the case for the past to be sure that it will have a place in the future.

The resulting political dialogue occurs in all societies. Every society contains its party of hope and party of memory and any society would be in trouble if either view were totally lost. The two perspectives often fight for control of the mind and heart of a single individual. Both positions are—or can be—grounded in the Christian faith. As Reinhold Niebuhr has reminded us, man has within himself the capacity for both incredible good and terrifying evil. Change, therefore, can be both creative and demonic. History partakes of this ambiguous character and the Christian attitude toward history shares in the ambiguity. The stand of the Christian on one side or another of the political dialogue is part of the ambiguity.

In politics, the liberal-conservative split is seen most sharply on the line where change is occurring. The liberal struggles always to advance—sometimes laboriously, against heavy odds, and with great impatience. The conservative tries to stand firm, convinced that the final change will be less drastic than it might have been had he not been there to man the ramparts. When the political wars are seen in this light, it ought to be clear that convinced and intelligent Christians can—and do—fight with integrity and compassion in either brigade.

But in spite of the liberal-conservative duality that is built into every political situation, American political parties do not reflect the dichotomy. The major parties are both nonideological. They may talk in ideological terms, but when a national election rolls around, they both scramble for the middle of the road, because there the votes are to be found.

The election of 1964 illustrates this point. The contest between Barry Goldwater and Lyndon B. Johnson had been anticipated as the great opportunity for Americans to choose between a liberal and a conservative candidate, a choice long obscured by the alleged me-too tactics of the Republican party. Yet, when the campaign unfolded, Goldwater spent his energies in trying to convince the public that all of those things he had said about Social Security and the TVA were not true, while Johnson presented himself as the moderate, efficient conserver of the American consensus. The 1964 campaign was especially disappointing to those who had believed that America was finally going to develop its own liberal and conservative parties, each with its own program for the nation. When the votes were counted, it seemed that the two-party system was just as confused ideologically as it had ever been. Perhaps it was merely a testimony to American political immaturity.

This analysis was sound, but the conclusion drawn from it was faulty. The 1964 election failed to divide the parties on ideological grounds. That failure, however, represented not an American weakness but, rather, a strength, for the result of ideological politics is polarization. When all the conservatives are in one party and all the liberals in the other, then politics loses its flexibility. Opponents find it hard to compromise because their position rests on conviction and principle, rather than on expediency. When the polarity becomes serious enough, it can divide the nation irreparably, as was the case in Germany in the 1920's, Spain in the 1930's, and the United States in 1860.

While Americans enjoy political argument and debate, they recognize that there is little fundamental cleavage in the nation's politics. At the basis of American life there is a great consensus and it is the job of the politicians to find that consensus and to identify themselves with it. Consequently, politics in America is seldom as divisive as it is in many other nations. If this is true, then how does Christian faith relate to political life? We have already suggested some of the ways in which Christians engage in politics. Let us see what lessons can be drawn from this participation.

THE RELIGIOUS DIMENSION OF POLITICS

First of all, Christians, whether they are Protestant or Catholic, do come to their political positions on the basis of their Christian faith. It would be naïve to assume that this is true of every church member who engages in politics but, let us admit, it is true more often than we realize. It must also be said, of course, that Christians seldom come to a political position on the basis of their Christian faith alone. A Christian does not exist in abstraction from the forces of his society. Other ingredients than religion are mixed into his views and the result is a blend of convictions, attitudes, preferences, and unconscious factors—many of them at odds with each other. Such is the way the human organism functions.

If this be true, then two corollaries follow. First, it is unreasonable to expect that Christians will find themselves always on the same side in politics and it is unwise, therefore, for the churches to make explicit demands upon their members to support specific legislation, candidates, or political parties. Second, the Christian who cares deeply about a specific issue or program cannot expect to carry his church along with him in support of his position. He has to accept the possibility that his bitterest political opponent may kneel down next to him at the Communion rail on Sunday and that his enemy has as much right to be there as he has himself.

Another insight that arises out of the nature of American politics is the realization that a Christian can be a loyal party man. This sounds like heresy, since political parties have never enjoyed much of a good reputation in church circles. But if we accept the fact that a political party is simply an instrument for discovering consensus, then we can see that its claims are merely organizational. American political parties, despite their high-sounding rhetoric, are not sacred societies. They make no absolute claims on their members that a Christian would have to reject. They are admittedly relative and secondary to the basic values. A man can afford to give himself to such a party because it can become for him a means for the realization of his own convictions. If he loses out in his party, he need not bolt the organization. He can simply wait and work for the day when his convictions again hold sway. Americans realize this better than they know. It is, in fact, why so few politicians ever leave their party. The party may require a great deal of loyalty, but the demand never reaches the depths of one's person. One seldom has to abandon one's fundamental convictions in order to stay aboard.

Finally, the nature of American politics is such as to enable the Christian to accept the political nature of politics. This may seem a strange way to state the case, but Christians have often mistaken ideology for politics and have supposed that being a Christian must mean the support of a specific agenda of Christian causes. Certainly, the Christian will have his causes to support, but he must beware of the trap of moralism. Moralism sets men apart from the opposition. It is stern and judgmental and tends to identify the opponent as the epitome of evil. Moralism makes no compromises because good cannot compromise with evil, nor virtue with vice. While causes have their place in politics—indeed, they are the content of politics—yet politics is the form and it has a logic of its own.

The essence of politics is compromise, moderation, and limit. The politician's role is to adjust conflicting claims, to moderate tensions, to produce substantial agreement out of a welter of conflicting causes. The politician never cuts himself off from his opponent for, even if he cannot convince him today, he may need his support another day. The politician does his most important work with his opponent, for the opponent is the source of possible compromise.

This attitude is more characteristically Christian than is the familiar stance of crusader. Christians believe that God alone is absolute. If this belief is taken seriously, it means that everything else in life is relative: our convictions, our political ideals, our visions of utopia, our position on this or that concrete issue. All are negotiable. The Christian doctrine of man is instructive at this point. "All have sinned and fall short of the glory of God," St. Paul tells us. It is easy to see how this applies to our political opponent whose wickedness and perversity are manifest. What is less easy to see is that we, too, are miserable sinners, incapable of any completely righteous and selfless act. Our best deeds, too, are mixed with unworthy motives and selfish interests. If we know this about ourselves and can understand and accept it, then we might find it just a little easier to do business with the sinner on the other side of the political fence. We might even find it possible to meet with him on the common ground of our mutual sinfulness. We can dare to compromise with him, even when our cherished convictions are involved because we know that our convictions are not absolute, not final ends in themselves.

Politics moves in the area of secondary principles, not ultimate values. It deals with the proximate end, the relative good, the temporary adjustment. The Christian can recognize the limited aims of political activity and refuse to permit the overextension of conflict. He will recognize that there are limits to conflict and that there are other persons like himself on the opposite side. He will realize that he has no right to degrade the opposition or to impugn their integrity and he will try, insofar as possible, to maintain personal contact with them.

For better or for worse, the United States Senate possesses this capacity for limited political warfare to an exceptional degree. There are ideological commitments in the Senate and there are personal disputes, often bitter ones. But one characteristic of this "most exclusive club in the world" is that, by and large, the members know each other and maintain fairly cordial personal relationships, even in the most bitter political battles. It sometimes causes consternation in the ranks of the followers when they discover that their favorite senator is a close personal friend of one of the leading members of the political opposition. Senators may call each other names in public, but they eat lunch together and, in general, try to keep on friendly terms. To the outsider, this all seems like a betrayal of virtue, as though these men were mere hypocrites. But to those who know how a legislative chamber operates, it seems only natural that men who have to work out knotty problems in legislation day after day should make some effort to keep on good terms with one another.

Let us not for a moment claim that the United States Senate provides a model of Christian love and brotherhood in action, nor suggest that the personal bond among senators is an outgrowth of their Christian profession. To explain their capacity for cordial personal relationships, we need look no further than to the political instinct which understands that today's enemy may be tomorrow's ally and that the real job of the politician is not to make ideological stands but to achieve the best results possible in the circumstances.

But this ability to work with the opposition, to subordinate conviction to expediency, to back water, and to compromise— this flexibility which is characteristic of the professional politician —is fully in accord with what we here conceive to be the stance of the responsible Christian in politics. For too long, Protestants have been beguiled by the crusader image. We have assumed that compromise contains the seeds of moral disintegration. We have assumed that somewhere there are Good Men who, if they could be lured into politics, would put an end to political shilly-shally-ing and would bring sincerity and honest convictions into the political arena. These are dangerous delusions. They tempt us to try to take the politics out of politics. To do this would be to remove the essential flexibility which makes a government work in a nation that contains approximately 180,000,000 political opinions.

So, to recapitulate, the old protest against religion intruding into politics has point to it. When in the past, Protestants have got involved in politics as Protestants—especially when the churches themselves have got involved—it has more often than not been an issue in which institutional interests were at stake. On the whole, the churches have not shown more insight or selflessness in the political arena than have the professional politicians.

Protestant activity in politics has been most creative when it has been centered around issues having to do with human welfare and values. In such cases, the political activity of committed churchmen has been supported and supplemented by other humanitarians who do not share the Protestant heritage. In spite of the prevailing conservatism of American Protestantism, this progressive tradition is still very much alive and active today.

Perhaps the most useful contribution of the Christian insight into politics is the new and growing understanding of the limits of ideology, convictions, and moral crusades. Politics is human interaction and Christians can contribute their understanding that the persons involved in the interaction are more significant than the ideas and the programs themselves.

Any statement about the relationship of religion and politics requires considerable analysis before it can be accepted or rejected. When someone calls for the church to "SPEAK OUT" on some issue of public concern, he may be crying out for moral leadership and guidance or he may merely be longing for the church to support him in a position that he has already arrived at on quite other grounds. Likewise, the claim that religion is a private affair which should not be mixed with politics may represent an attempt to relegate religion to the sphere of inward piety, making faith impotent and politically irresponsible. Or again, it may be a plea for independence from ideological and ecclesiastical rigidity, a call for freedom of judgment that will enable political men to relativize their conflicts and make them bearable.

3 FROM MISSION TO REALISM
IN WORLD AFFAIRS

AMERICA'S RELATIONS with the rest of the world constitute a major theme in her national life. Since about the turn of the century, the United States has participated in world affairs as one of the major powers. Greatness was suddenly thrust upon the nation as a consequence of the logic of industrialism and the expansion of trade and communications, all of which took place largely between the close of the Civil War and the beginning of the war with Spain. While foreign affairs were not new to the nation, after 1900 they began to exert far more influence than ever before. In the twentieth century, foreign policy has been a leading theme in most presidential elections, except perhaps those from 1928 to 1936.

The Protestant churches naturally responded to this new challenge to the Christian social ethic. The first reactions of churchmen to foreign affairs were relatively uncritical and undistinguished. As time went on, there developed a specifically Christian moral critique of international relations, a critique that was, in turn, subjected to a more incisive and penetrating analysis.

The focus of Christian concern in international relations has, of course, been the problem of war with its accompanying bloodshed, destruction, hatred, and repression. There had been already, on the American scene, a peace movement which was focused in the American Peace Society and went back to the early nineteenth century. The peace movement was normally supported by the historic peace churches such as the Mennonites, the Brethren, and the Friends. The rest of Protestantism showed little interest in the problem, though many church leaders expressed confidence that great wars were a thing of the past. The peace movement occasionally enjoyed some small measure of approval during periods of international calm, but when war threatened or actually broke out, the churches almost always supported the war and bitterly attacked those who remained loyal to the cause of peace.

What was the basis for the churches' renunciation of the peace movement? The specific grounds varied from time to time, but they can be summed up in Professor Ralph Gabriel's phrase, "the mission of America." [1] Americans have long maintained the conviction that this nation is peculiarly called to exert its energies in order to dispense justice and to right international wrongs. The attitude has varied in its intensity and self-confidence, but it has been a persistent feature of the American consciousness and it has been shared and propagated by the Protestant churches.

THE ERA OF EXPANSION

This missionary conception of American foreign policy can be seen in its purest form at the time when the country was first waking to its position as a world power. Within a single decade, the United States fought a war against one of the traditional

European powers and emerged with territories in the Caribbean and in the Far East; it acquired the Hawaiian Islands; it extracted permission, over Colombian protests, to build a canal across the Isthmus of Panama; and it began to exercise a kind of suzerainty over the whole of Latin America. Thus a massive shift occurred in the historic relationship of the United States to other nations. A self-contained, continental nation had become an aggressive participant in the game of world imperialism.

Protestants reacted to this shift in a way that was both surprising and predictable. This period of American history probably represents the zenith of Protestant America, with its view of a continuity between American culture and the Christian religion, Protestant version. Leading churchmen were leading citizens. Protestants saw themselves as standing at the very center of the national life. American policies were, ipso facto, Protestant policies and there was no apology for the fact. Therefore, while it might seem curious that Christians should so readily accept war, naval expansion, toughness, and aggressiveness in foreign affairs, the churches' relation to the culture at that time made their support of public policy inevitable.

The Protestant apologetic for expansionism was a combination of national interest and national responsibility. The Rev. Dr. Josiah Strong, popular author and executive secretary of the interdenominational Evangelical Alliance, articulated the case for national interest. He saw that, as a result of America's industrial and commercial vitality, excess American capital would increasingly go abroad and Americans would acquire interests all over the world. Consequently, the United States would become dependent on foreign markets which would then have to be protected. "This is a commercial age," he wrote, "and commercial considerations are the mainspring of national policies." [2] There are striking echoes of Marx and anticipations of Lenin in that statement. The sole difference is that Strong approved of the process, while Marx and Lenin denounced it.

From our superior vantage point of today, it seems curious that Strong was critical of the ills of American society and was a leader in the movement to bring the Christian message to bear on the evils of urban life in America. When it came to viewing the world scene, however, he accepted the crassest values of business civilization without questioning them. The key to this paradox lies in the doctrine of race that underlay so much of American thought of that period. Strong, like many other Americans, was convinced that the Anglo-Saxon "race" was superior, not only in vitality and accomplishments, but in morality as well. He envisioned American power and influence sweeping over all the world. The result would be beneficial to the lesser races because they would be given the superior values and institutions of Anglo-Saxon culture, particularly democratic government and Protestant Christianity.[3] Thus the argument based on national interest shades off into an argument based on moral uplift.

A similar view was enunciated by Lyman Abbott, noted preacher, author, editor, and generally liberal voice on the Protestant scene. Writing shortly after the turn of the century, Abbott proclaimed it the duty of the advanced race to spread the benefits of civilization to the barbarians, even if it hurt. He declared:

> It is the function of the Anglo-Saxon Race to confer those gifts of civilization through law, commerce and education, on the uncivilized peoples of the world. If we are to do this, we must begin with law uttered with authority and enforced by power. We cannot confer law on a recalcitrant people without evil; we cannot do it, as men are constituted, without some measure of hardship and injustice.[4]

The doctrine of the inequality of races made it possible to recognize human sinfulness in the uncivilized peoples while ignoring its persistence among superior Anglo-Saxons.

The effect on actual policies of this moral interpretation of American imperialism may be most clearly seen in President William McKinley's own statement regarding his agonized decision, after a long period of doubt and hesitation, to keep the Philippine Islands as an American possession. To a group of visiting clergymen, McKinley described how he had spent a night in prayer and then it was given to him to see his duty. He saw that he could not return the islands to Spanish misrule. He could not turn them over to America's competitors, Britain or France. Nor would it be responsible to turn them loose, since they were obviously incapable of self-government. "There was nothing left for us to do but to take them all and to educate the Filipinos, and uplift and Christianize them, and by God's grace do the very best we could by them, as our fellowmen for whom Christ also died." [5]

There is no reason to doubt McKinley's sincerity. He was only interpreting his actions in the same way that America's new foreign policy was being interpreted in Protestant pulpits throughout the land. Like the preachers, he was aware of the political and commercial aspects of imperialism, but like them too, he regarded the moral dimension as paramount. Hence, American imperialism did not come under critical theological analysis because it was seen as part and parcel of the Protestant mission to the world.

Indeed the Protestant mission entered the discussion of expansionism in even more direct ways. Protestant missionaries were already operating in various areas throughout the world. Almost to a man, the missionaries expected American protection while overseas and hoped for the expansion of American power as a way of opening up new territories to the advance of the missionary movement. At no point in American history is there more clearly evident a functional breakdown in the traditional relationship of church and state. Just as businessmen were later to demand United States government intervention to save their foreign properties from expropriation, so the Protestant missionaries called on their government to enforce upon other nations guarantees of religious freedom that would make their work possible. They demanded government action to save missionaries from hostile action by the governments and peoples of the lands to which they journeyed. The missionary impulse thus gave a powerful motive to demands for American expansion, demands that came not only from the missionaries themselves, but from the churches at home that sent them out.

There was some opposition to this new movement, to be sure. The Rt. Rev. Henry C. Potter, Episcopal Bishop of New York, criticized the Spanish-American War in his 1898 Convention Address, given shortly after the close of the war. He also opposed American acquisition of the Philippines. He withdrew this opposition only after he visited the islands in 1899 and decided for himself that they were not yet ready for self-government.[6]

Aside from Bishop Potter, the Congregational clergyman and author Washington Gladden was almost the only other major Protestant figure who spoke out against the war. At this time, Gladden was widely known and respected for his liberal social views. He finally gave his support to the war but did so only with great reluctance. While in England in the summer of 1898, he justified American entry into war on humanitarian grounds but, believing the declaration of war to have been hasty and ill-advised, he gave no unqualified blessing to the enterprise. In his memoirs, written a decade later, he gave a judicious and balanced account of his views in retrospect. Admitting that various evil motives entered into the choice for war: greed, ambition, jingoism, race hatred, religious bigotry, yet he wrote, "I am sure . . . that the final word for war was spoken by the impulse of humanity . . . but those who spoke it were ill-informed about the attitude of the Spanish government." He went on to express his doubts whether "President McKinley gave the people all the information they ought to have had in that critical moment." [7]

WORLD WAR I

The American attitude toward the lesser civilizations of the Pacific area continued to be one of benevolent and paternalistic superiority as American influence increased in both China and Japan as well as in the Philippines. At the same time, the national attitude toward Europe, always somewhat ambiguous, was slowly becoming redefined under the stress of the fear of impending war.

When war finally came in 1914, it found a fairly vital peace movement in existence in the United States. The peace feeling was composed of a number of related factors, including a recognition of commercial interdependence, a genuine horror of the inhumanity of warfare, a contempt for the bickering of the European states, and a recognition of the variety of European backgrounds of the American population. Whatever genuine isolationism existed was based on the conviction that American interests would best be served by remaining aloof from the European power struggle.

This position was a minority view, if not in 1914 then at least by 1917 when America entered the war. In spite of President Woodrow Wilson's call for neutrality of thought as well as deed, most Americans were never truly neutral. The preponderant tradition was one of identification with Britain as the "mother country" even on the part of many whose ancestry was not British. In addition, Allied propaganda had circulated stories of German atrocities, tending to support the view that the real purpose of the war was to defend democracy against the attacks of a brutal Prussian militarism. By 1917, most of the nation was convinced that the war was a struggle against the forces of evil and darkness and that American entry would save the world for democracy in a war to end all war.

Up to the time that America actually went to war, there was a genuine dialogue within Protestantism over the issue of war or peace. The historic peace churches continued their tradition of opposition to all war, but their witness was blunted because they included in their numbers many citizens of German descent whose opposition to the British war propaganda could easily be interpreted as disloyal sentiment. Walter Rauschenbusch, the acknowledged leader of the social gospel movement, opposed the war, thereby helping to bring the issue of war and peace for the first time onto the social gospel agenda. A Church Peace Union was formed before the outbreak of war in 1914. During the years of American neutrality, it sought to mobilize antiwar sentiment.

During the same period, interventionist groups endeavored to arouse support for American preparedness. While America's actual entry into the war was seldom discussed, it hovered in the background as a likely possibility. Britain's cause was identified with that of the Almighty and opponents to preparedness were denounced as traitors. By the time war was actually declared, emotions had reached a fever pitch and all rational discussion of the issue was effectively closed off.

At no time in American history has the identification of national policy with the Divine Will been stated more baldly than in those days when America entered World War I. Wilson's justification of the war on democratic and humanitarian grounds was exceeded by the preachers who saw it in terms of the sacred. Thus, the Rev. Dr. Henry Churchill King, President of Oberlin College, was able to affirm, "It is neither a travesty nor exaggeration to call this war on the part of America a truly Holy War." [8] The Rev. Dr. Randolph McKim, prominent rector of the Episcopal Church of the Epiphany in Washington, went further, saying, "It is God who has summoned us to this war. It is his war we are fighting. . . . This contest is indeed a crusade. The greatest in history—the holiest. It is in the profoundest and truest sense a Holy War." [9]

Since God had demanded participation in his war, he would undoubtedly guarantee the results and vindicate the methods of warfare. Congregations were assured by their clergy that their boys would find God in the trenches, that they were being led by fine Christian gentlemen, and that Christ himself would, if he were here, be found fighting along with them. As one YMCA leader put it, "He [Christ] would take the bayonet and grenade and bomb and rifle and do the work of deadliness against that which is the most deadly enemy of his Father's kingdom in a thousand years. . . . That is the inexorable truth about Jesus Christ and this war; and we rejoice to say it." [10]

These quotations are not isolated instances of clergy who were particularly insensitive to the moral issues involved in total war. They are representative of the thinking of the vast majority of the Protestant clergy. The conviction that the war was a crusade, that good and evil could be readily translated into Allied and German, was widespread. It is clear that the Protestant churches invested considerable emotional and moral capital in the war. The corresponding letdown after the war was a foregone conclusion.

INTERWAR PACIFISM

The postwar disillusionment was serious and long-lasting. Indeed, it persisted well into the 1930's and paralyzed Protestant thinking about foreign affairs until the coming of the next war. Protestants were shocked and disturbed by the revelations of the secret wartime treaties of the Allies, by the Allies' cynical disregard for Wilson's high aims at the peace conference, by the results of the study into German war guilt, by the disclosure of the unreliability of many of the wartime atrocity stories—in sum, by the realization that the war, far from being holy, was merely one more European power struggle, such as America had traditionally tried to avoid.

The result of this disillusionment was a new wave of pacifism that swept over Protestantism and the nation as a whole. It included a number of ingredients, not always consciously related to one another. One factor was the sheer horror of modern war, which had been disclosed for the first time in World War I. Shrapnel, poison gas, air raids, and mass destruction entered the military scene and the resulting casualty lists staggered the imagination. But deeper than the horror was the futility of war. Far from being a crusade for God and country, war came to be seen as a cynical struggle for domination of colonies, markets, and territories. The Versailles Treaty proved that idealistic aims were no more than a cover for motives of national aggrandizement.

The antiwar impulse entered into the liberal critique of American society. It was coupled with a general denunciation of imperialism, foreign entanglements, military spending, large armies and navies, and military training in colleges. While most of this criticism emanated from the social gospel wing of Protestantism, it was echoed in all quarters because it struck a responsive chord in the war-weariness of Americans of whatever political or theological persuasion. The mood was reflected in American willingness to limit the size of the United States Navy at the Washington Naval Conference and in the signing of the Kellogg-Briand Pact which was intended to outlaw war for all time. Even American reluctance to enter the League of Nations can best be explained as a result of the nation's fear of being dragged into another foreign war because of its commitment to the League.

There is an old saying that the generals are always found adequately prepared to fight the last war, but not the one coming up. The same could be said of the theologians. The disenchantment with World War I was no doubt well grounded but it was little help to a generation that faced the challenge of Nazi Germany. Having learned of the exaggerations of the World War I atrocity stories, Americans were ill-prepared to face the realities of Nazi brutality. Having been misled in the past by stories of enemy plans for aggression and domination, Americans were ill-prepared to recognize such attempts when they actually appeared. President Franklin D. Roosevelt saw the threat earlier than did most churchmen and he began to prepare the country to meet it. The chief obstacle to the increasing internationalism of his foreign policy was pacifist-oriented Protestantism.

The 1930's brought a series of crises that rocked the system of collective security envisioned by the League of Nations and left the League a shambles. Japanese movements into Manchuria in 1931 and into China in 1937; the Italian invasion of Ethiopia in 1936; the Spanish civil war and, finally, Hitler's aggressive moves into Austria and Czechoslovakia traced a pattern that spelled imminent war. While each of these events caused some uneasiness in the United States, it was not until the Munich agreement of October, 1938, that the American public began to come to terms with the possibility of war. Indeed, Munich represents something of an emotional crisis for Americans, for the memory of Munich is still invoked whenever the question of negotiation with an antagonist is discussed.

By and large, liberal Christians of the social gospel variety opposed any indication of American military preparedness. The *Christian Century,* which had considered Roosevelt too conservative to merit its support in 1932, had come to accept the New Deal with enthusiasm by 1936. Yet, by 1940, the *Christian Century* had broken with the President because of his famous "Quarantine Speech" of 1937 in which he had pointed to the increase of international lawlessness and had declared that, like a disease, it must be kept from spreading. Though Roosevelt pledged America to keeping the peace, he hinted that the nation would have to maintain a position that would not encourage aggressors to break the peace. The *Christian Century* approved of the moral tone of the speech, but voiced fear of its implications for future international activity. As time went on, suspicion of Roosevelt's motives was increased by the debates in Congress over the neutrality acts and, after war broke out in Europe, over Lend-Lease. Most of all, liberal Protestants objected to the plans for a peacetime military draft.[11]

WORLD WAR II

Opposition to a military build-up was not based exclusively on either isolationism or irresponsibility, as is often charged. There was a sincere conviction that America's best contribution to world peace was in the sphere of moral leadership rather than power politics. It assumed that the powerful nations of the world would be swayed by the force of world opinion when that opinion was uttered in clear moral tones. On a less optimistic level, there were also those who, while recognizing fully the course of European affairs, realized that it was far too late to prevent war and that, if America attempted to prevent it, then America would be sucked into the vortex of war and the result would be complete international chaos.

It was at this point that Reinhold Niebuhr broke definitely with his social gospel antecedents and attempted to restore a measure of realism and responsibility into the American Protestant political consciousness. Niebuhr had long ago separated himself from the pacifist Fellowship of Reconciliation because he refused to absolutize the repudiation of violence. Niebuhr was far from advocating anything like a holy war. His sense of the depth of human sinfulness would hardly permit that. Yet, while recognizing the sins and limitations of all forms of political power, he maintained that the differences between the Western democracies and Nazi Germany were real and important. Political man, in Niebuhr's view, is called to make responsible choices from among the possibilities that history offers him. To refuse to prepare for war is not to ensure peace, but to ensure the victory of the aggressor. While war is undoubtedly evil, it may prove to be the lesser of two evils.

Late in 1941, before the United States entered the war, Niebuhr and a number of colleagues, including John C. Bennett, John Mackay, Douglas Horton, and Bishop Henry Knox Sherrill, brought out a new journal called *Christianity and Crisis* to bring their views to the attention of the churches. In their prospectus, they gave their reasons:

> In the conflicts in Europe and Asia, ethical issues are at stake which claim the sympathy and support of American Christians. . . . When men and nations must choose between two great evils, the choice of the lesser evil becomes their duty. We hold that the halting of totalitarian aggression is prerequisite to world peace and order.[12]

Under the impact of Niebuhr's articulate and impassioned cry for responsibility, Protestant pacifism began to decline. It may be too much to credit Niebuhr with effecting the change singlehandedly. Certainly other voices besides his were often raised. Yet his was perhaps the most influential and respected single voice and, what is more, he spoke to the most sensitive and informed of the younger clergy, many of whom were already his theological disciples. At any rate, Niebuhr's brand of thinking is stamped on the whole Protestant attitude toward the war, even after America entered into it. If Niebuhr did not shape that response, he at least articulated it in sound, theological terms.

For, contrary to the period of World War I, there was little of the holy war sentiment in the churches' attitude toward World War II. Government propaganda to the contrary, few churchmen saw the struggle as anything other than a nasty and regrettable business. While there was less opposition to the war, there was also less persecution of dissenters. Pacifists were relatively well treated. Special camps and duties were provided for conscientious objectors. Religious scruples were carefully observed. Hitler and Hirohito provided convenient symbols for hate campaigns, but relatively little violent anti-German or anti-Japanese feeling was expressed in church circles. Indeed, in the only genuine domestic atrocity, the relocation of the West Coast Japanese-Americans into concentration camps, the churches quickly responded by providing ministries and relief to the affected people.[13]

On the other hand, World War II demonstrated that America's alleged moral superiority is a dangerous myth. Once in the war, the United States pursued victory relentlessly, almost completely without moral restraint. Saturation bombing of Germany and fire-bombing of vulnerable Japanese cities added immensely to the already burdensome total of civilian casualties. The American conscience became so conditioned to destruction and brutality that it was even able to accept, without any great revulsion, the explosion of atomic bombs over Hiroshima and Nagasaki.

The debate has raged for twenty years over whether the two atomic bombs had to be dropped or whether some other means could have been found to bring the war with Japan to an end.[14] The use of the bombs is usually defended on the ground that they forced Japan to an early surrender, thereby averting a costly invasion of the Japanese Islands. This argument fails to explain why a second atomic bomb was dropped on Nagasaki only three days after the Hiroshima attack. The brief interval gave the

Japanese government almost no time in which to make a diplomatic response to the first shock. Then too, the precipitous haste
with which the bombs were used (only three weeks elapsed
between the first successful test of the atomic bomb in New
Mexico and its first use at Hiroshima) suggests that little time
was spent searching for alternatives. The entry of the U.S.S.R.
into the Japanese war certainly offered such an alternative. The
Soviet Union had already agreed to enter the war no later than
August 8, 1945. There are indications that the Soviet offensive
had as much to do with the Japanese decision to surrender as did
the atomic bombs.[15] Thus a delay of only one week might have
made the use of the atomic bomb unnecessary.

Apologists for the use of the atomic bombs have frequently
pointed out that the fire-bombing of Japanese cities had already
killed far more people than were lost at Hiroshima and Nagasaki.
They are right, of course. The atomic bomb itself merely serves
as a poignant symbol of the lengths to which an otherwise hu-
mane and civilized people can be carried in the midst of total
war. It was the single-minded preoccupation with total victory
that gradually paralyzed American moral sensitivities, making
possible both the indiscriminate fire-bombing and the atomic
bomb attacks. The result was an almost unbelievable escalation
of horror and slaughter. Movement toward the achievement of
peace through diplomacy was, at the same time, rendered nearly
impossible just when it was most likely to succeed.[16]

Thus the United States has been no more successful in dealing
with the ethical perplexities of war than has any other nation.
Whatever immediate benefits the atomic bomb attacks may have
brought in 1945, the fact remains that the United States will
henceforth be remembered as the nation which first used man's
most awful weapon of destruction. In this sense, the spirit of
Hiroshima and Nagasaki hangs over the postwar world like a dark
cloud, making it hard for the world at large to see with any clarity
the moral superiority of America.

POSTWAR INTERNATIONALISM

The war transformed the United States into a fully committed participant in world affairs, not by choice but by necessity. Americans had long regarded international crises as "problems" to be "solved." From now on the situation was going to be different, as Secretary of State Dean Acheson pointed out in 1946:

> Our name for these problems is significant. We call them headaches. You take a powder and they are gone. These pains are not like that. They are like the pain of earning a living. They will stay with us until death. We have got to understand that all our lives the danger, the uncertainty, the need for alertness, for effort, for discipline will be upon us.[17]

There were two principal reasons for America's new sense of world responsibility. The United States was now the most powerful country in the postwar world, having suffered comparatively less war damage than any other major nation. Then too, Soviet Russia emerged from its isolation to provide serious obstacles to the reconstruction of Europe on a democratic base. The Soviet threat called for a unified response by the Western nations. The preponderant power of the United States made it the leader of that response.

As the nation adjusted to its new internationalism, most Protestants abandoned what isolationism still remained. Even so, Protestant churchmen divided on nearly every major issue in foreign affairs. Conservatives, appealing to the image of Protestant America, were inclined to nationalism, militarism, and anticommunism. Progressives were more disposed to favor multilateral actions and were oriented toward economic rather than military solutions.

The United Nations enjoyed the approval of most progressive

Protestants. To the hopeful, it was a path to the "one world" of the future while, to the less optimistic, it was at least a responsible effort to keep the peace. Some supporters of the United Nations have tended to overvalue its legal and organizational machinery to the neglect of the underlying power factors which actually determine the course of international politics. The vicissitudes of the United Nations' peacekeeping efforts have consequently produced some frustration and anxiety among the organization's most ardent Protestant advocates.

Conservative Protestants have generally expressed concern over the United Nations on the ground that it limits American sovereignty. They believe, predictably, that America can best preserve peace and freedom throughout the world without the aid of other, presumably less moral, nations.

The foreign aid program, America's most radical postwar innovation in foreign policy, is generally supported by progressive Protestants in the name of Christian charity. They tend to be suspicious of the large amount of military assistance that has become an integral part of the program. They likewise deplore the use of economic assistance as a bribe or a threat to a wavering ally. Conservative Protestants see the program chiefly as a weapon in the anticommunist struggle and welcome the emphasis on military assistance. In contrast to the progressives, they are more likely to advocate the use of foreign aid funds to "help our friends—only."

The cold war has dominated American foreign policy in recent years. In no area of American life has the cleavage in Protestantism been so pronounced as in the reaction to this ideological confrontation. Conservatives have given the old "holy war" terminology a new lease on life; Soviet Russia is denounced in unreserved terms as the epitome of totalitarianism, terrorism, atheism, and materialism. The mission of America is interpreted as the task of saving the world from communism. At the height of the cold-war tension, every nation in the world was called upon to take its stand on one side or the other. Those which opted for the traditional American position of "proud neutrality" were castigated as fools or enemies.

During most of the cold-war period, progressive Protestantism was weak, divided, and on the defensive. The embattled position of all liberals in the United States was illustrated by the activities of the House Un-American Activities Committee, the power of the federal government's loyalty-security program, and the antics of Senator Joseph R. McCarthy. Any progressive idea was likely to be labeled as disloyal. There was a hint of the old revivalist theology in this brand of anticommunism. Good and evil, like the saved and the unsaved, were conceived of as separate and distinguishable. America is good; Russia is bad. Protestant Christianity is good; communism is bad. Liberal political views shade off into socialism and ultimately into communism, so they too are bad.

Most progressive Protestants were themselves anticommunist, though many of them resented the demand that they prove their loyalty to the nation. They tended to reject the simple black-and-white moral categories in which conservatives interpreted the issues. They were also likely to be less rigid in their opposition to the Soviet Union, more open to negotiation with the communists and generally suspicious of rhetoric about "liberating" the nations under communist rule.

In spite of their obvious divergence in specific areas, both conservative and progressive Protestants continue to maintain the doctrine of the mission of America. Conservatives see this mission as the unilateral activity of a strong and moral America that will eventually destroy communism and bring world peace. Foreign policy easily lapses into the vocabulary of the crusader for, to this kind of Protestant, the anticommunist struggle is a crusade. To progressives, the mission of America is to provide economic assistance to the underdeveloped nations in order to raise their standard of living. They look toward the eventual establishment of American social democracy throughout the world by the free choice of the common people.

Both positions also retain a substantial degree of moralism. For the conservative, America is moral and the rest of the world must be taught to live up to her high standard. The progressive is more likely to maintain that America is not moral enough. Somehow the nation is expected to preserve its world leadership by virtue of its own moral achievement, providing, thereby, an example for the rest of the world to follow.

Developments on the world scene, meanwhile, threaten to make obsolete the attitudes of both parties. As a result of the nuclear stalemate and the development of intercontinental ballistic missiles, a new diplomacy has begun to emerge. It requires a strong military capacity, a nuclear arsenal, a willingness to use limited force, and a readiness to maneuver in such a way as to leave both sides room for flexibility and compromise.

Protestants have not yet developed any consistent response to this new set of conditions. Conservatives accept the need for armaments but chafe at the limitations imposed upon their use. Progressives welcome the reduction of ideological tensions and the consequent willingness to negotiate with the communists, but they have not adjusted to the continued need to rely on military power. Both viewpoints are likely to undergo considerable modification in future years as the nation grows in maturity and restraint.

In this continually changing atmosphere, the official attitude of most major Protestant church bodies has been largely a progressive one. They have generally approved the nation's movement toward internationalism, while frequently raising questions about specific aspects of American foreign policy. The churches have shared in the national government's anticommunist stance, its espousal of economic assistance as an instrument of foreign policy, and its commitment to an expanded program of national defense. President Harry Truman received the support of the churches at the outbreak of the Korean War, while President Dwight D. Eisenhower was similarly supported in his goal of bringing the war to a close.

Since World War II, some Protestant churches, either singly

or in concert, have developed extensive programs of education for international responsibility. They have dealt with such issues as arms control, new forms of warfare and nonmilitary coercion, economic development and collective security. Unfortunately, little has been done as yet to evaluate the effectiveness of these ventures. Conferences are held, papers read, books published, and study groups formed, but no one knows whether or not these activities have any substantial impact upon the participants. There are signs, in Protestant circles, of a growing political maturity that is reflected in the attitude of ordinary Protestant churchmen toward world affairs. It would be too much, however, to claim that this maturation is a result of the churches' own educational efforts. The greater impact may very likely be that of the mass communications media: radio, television, newspapers, and the national magazines.

THE PROPHETIC ROLE OF THE CHURCHES

The churches have a special responsibility to speak to the issues of international relations because they involve war and peace, life and death. Support and criticism of government policies are necessary, often both at the same time. The United Nations deserves support, for example, though churchmen ought to be aware that the United Nations is only an instrument, no better than the purposes it serves. In spite of the limitations of the organization, the United States should be encouraged to continue to take a responsible part in making it an effective instrument for keeping the peace.

Foreign aid likewise deserves consistent, though not unreserved, support. Christians must recognize the practical limitations of economic assistance, though churchmen should have no difficulty in endorsing the principle that America's abundance ought to be shared with the less fortunate. On a more practical level, they can raise their voices in support of adequate funds for the program. The decisions as to how the money is to be used most effectively can be left to the experts.

The churches can contribute to the formulation of wise and mature foreign policy by bringing to bear on international relations their own theological insights. If we are genuinely committed to the biblical understanding of man as sinner, we can at least see that we have something in common with our enemies. If we know ourselves to be, like them, mere sinful human beings, we will recognize that we can do business with them. If we are convinced that only God is absolute, we can accept the relativity of all political arrangements and will then be able to resign ourselves to the settlement of specific disputes, resisting the temptation to demand final and total solutions.

It might also be possible for the churches to help policymakers to face the unresolved fuzziness of much of America's thinking about foreign affairs. Americans have come to accept the view that policy must be based on the realities of power, but have not worked out the relationship between the use of power in carrying out policy and the ethical ends of policy. Americans agree now that national self-interest constitutes a legitimate goal of foreign policy, but have not adequately defined what is meant by valid national interest. Moreover, Americans are still reluctant to concede the right of national self-interest to other nations, either their allies or their enemies. And while they have long since decided that they ought to intervene to help weaker neighbors, Americans have not come to terms with the limits of that doctrine in any meaningful way. The perplexities of our current military intervention in South Vietnam provide a convincing illustration of this point.

At the same time, the churches' prophetic criticism of foreign policy continues to be important, for Americans have not yet learned to live with the ambiguities and the uncertainties of international politics. Reinhold Niebuhr taught his countrymen a reluctant acceptance of the use of force and violence in the name of grim necessity. Less sensitive men can easily pervert this point of view into an enthusiastic espousal of force with an overlay of moral pronouncement. American thinking about international affairs is still bound by the categories of the thirties. Like the generals, the average citizen thinks in terms of the last war, identifying an abstraction called "communism" with the Hitler-demon of the past and seeing every negotiation as "appeasement."

In this confused climate of opinion, foreign policies are often packaged and sold to a gullible public by means of fancy labels and slogans. The nation is thus led to support reckless military adventures and the costly retention of useless and exposed positions all over the world. America's undoubted military might makes it easy to convince her people that any problem of power can be solved by sending in the Marines. Her economic bounty tempts her people to believe that they can buy friends and buy off enemies. Her reluctance to endorse any overseas adventure can be overcome by pointing to the spread of communism and appealing to the reliable "Munich syndrome."

Even more disturbing is the growing reluctance to engage in free and open discussion of the issues. Though Americans still speak in theoretical terms of the fact that democracy thrives on criticism, whenever a real crisis occurs and a controversial step is taken, criticism is denounced in the name of patriotism and the need to present a united front to the world. Americans are told that their leaders deserve their support because the leaders know more than the average person does.

The independence of the churches in the political realm gives them the means to combat this benevolent authoritarianism. Their critical task is to see that the right questions are asked and the real issues faced. Of course, theologians and lay Christians are not necessarily experts in foreign affairs, nor do they have to be. They need only be intelligent and sensitive interpreters and critics of national policies. Statesmen who are genuinely committed to the high goals of peace and justice for all men will have no trouble defending themselves from this kind of criticism. Indeed, they will benefit from it, for it well help to save them from the myopia that so easily affects the vision of the administrator who is too close to a policy and too committed to its success to be able to see it in long-range perspective.

Christian critics of national policies need not demand the impossible. We have learned that moral perfection is not possible in the area of statecraft. We have learned something of the moral ambiguities inherent in the uses of power. We have learned that we must "render unto Caesar." But we must retain our ethical sensitivity in meeting Caesar's demands. As one political moralist has stated the case, "Give unto Caesar? Of course, but with a tragic sense of necessity, not with the vulgar joy of Caesar's fellow-traveller." [18]

4 GODLINESS, THE SCHOOLS, AND
   THE AMERICAN CONSENSUS

THE RELATIONSHIP of religion and the educational process has always been a subject of controversy in America, bound up as it is with the problem of church-state separation. Education is one of the functions traditionally ascribed to the church, but in modern times it has almost wholly passed into public control under the aegis of the state. The process has been a slow one through the years, but it has been steady. Controversy over the proper role of church and state has always taken place at the edge of change, with the forces of religion ever retreating before the advancing forces of state operation and control.

In education, this process has not always resulted in struggle and antipathy. The churches have generally recognized that, in America, free common schools must necessarily fall under public control. Most American churchmen, even those who support their own private or church schools, have tended to approve the prin-

ciple of the public school, though they often differ strongly over
how the school ought to carry out its task. Since the church occupied a position under the old scheme of things which it no
longer occupies, it is only natural that the forces of religion have
often defended the older ways against the new. As a result, the
churches have been inclined to conservatism in the area of education, often equating the forces of change with the forces of god-
lessness. It is easy to equate the presence of God in the schools
with the presence of a highly visible ecclesiastical establishment.

No discussion of religion in education would be complete without some consideration of the practices of the past and the
changes which have already been made in the place of religion in
the American school. While this subject itself is important enough
to warrant a major treatment, it might still be worthwhile to
sketch a brief picture of some of the pivotal changes that have
occurred in the relationship of religion to the schools.

THE NINETEENTH-CENTURY CONSENSUS

The original American colonies had no uniform system of education and almost no legal provisions for schooling at all. Massachusetts alone required the towns to maintain schools, but the
requirements could easily be evaded—and were, more often than
not. Massachusetts, however, was at least far enough along the
road to providing something which could be called public education that it seems appropriate to single out that colony for special
attention.

Each town in Massachusetts was supposed to provide for a
schoolteacher. While the town government itself was to provide
the funds, the local church had the right to oversee the school,
the minister usually being the overseer. As time went on, con-
cessions were made to citizens who were not members of the
established Congregational Church and there was less ecclesiastical control of the school. After the Revolution, the towns were

still required to provide teachers of the Protestant religion, which for all practical purposes meant the established church. The minister no longer controlled education, but he still, as a rule, served on the board of overseers.

By mid-nineteenth century, Massachusetts was emerging as the undisputed leader in American public education with the appointment of Horace Mann as state superintendent of schools. For the first time, a statewide system was being developed under public control. Mann moved to raise the level of teaching and to develop professional standards for the entire state. His work was to provide a model for the rest of the nation as it entered the period of its greatest expansion in public education.

For this reason, Mann's view of the place of religion in public education is especially significant. He worked within the context of church-state separation, inasmuch as Massachusetts already forbade sectarian teaching in the public schools, although no attempt had been made to prevent the teaching of religion of a nonsectarian sort. Part of Mann's task as superintendent was to make sure that attempts to introduce sectarian teaching into the schools were resisted. He was largely successful in this enterprise and, as a result, was held by some churchmen to be opposed to the teaching of religion at all.

While accepting the need to forbid sectarian teaching, Mann nonetheless wanted to maintain the religious character of the public schools. This was easier said than done, since most of the available books on religion were full of slanted, doctrinaire, sectarian instruction. Mann succeeded in barring most of this literature from the schools while retaining moral instruction based on the Bible itself. He defended his views in his final report of 1848:

I believed then, as now, that religious instruction in our schools, to the extent that the Constitution and the laws of the State allowed and prescribed, was indispensable to their highest welfare, and essential to the vitality of moral education. . . . Our system earnestly inculcates all Christian morals; it founds its morals on the basis of religion; it welcomes the religion of the Bible; and in receiving the Bible, it allows it to do what it is allowed to do in no other system, to speak for itself.[1]

By "speaking for itself," Mann was referring to the practice of reading the Bible without comment, in order to avoid any sectarian interpretation. This practice found wide favor and was used in many states until the recent United States Supreme Court decision which found the practice unconstitutional.

Mann was interested in the teaching of religion as an aid to morality. Thus he would emphasize ethical injunctions and the example of Jesus, without any theological interpretation. He referred contemptuously to "man-made" dogmatic theology, which he contrasted unfavorably with the sublimity of the biblical ethic itself.

To present-day readers, Mann's solution may seem a bit naïve, but for his time and place it was the obvious course of action. The atmosphere of Massachusetts was Christian in a general way. The main religious bodies ranged from orthodox Calvinists to Unitarians. Roman Catholics were beginning to arrive in force, but they were not yet a potent political factor. There were few Jews. Such unbelievers as existed evidently found it prudent to keep their views to themselves. There was what might be called a "Christian consensus," at least on the moral and ethical level. It was only natural that this consensus should have been expressed and made manifest in the public schools.

The naïveté of the arrangement lies in its easy acceptance of ethics as the heart of Christianity. Biblical theology in our own time has laid the groundwork for a powerful reassertion of the gospel proclamation as the heart of the Christian faith. Jesus' ethical teachings are important, but they are not to be equated with the gospel. Indeed, the heavy stress laid on ethics tended to produce a Protestant moralism, a new version of justification by works which interprets Christianity as a new law with no gospel at all.

In spite of its theological shortcomings, the settlement seemed to satisfy the needs of society. Educators agreed that ethical religion could be taught in the public schools. The nonsectarian version of Christianity became something like an established religion of the school system. The settlement was unstable and sooner or later was sure to be challenged, but so long as it answered the felt needs of the society, it would last.

BREAKDOWN OF THE CONSENSUS

A challenge to the nonsectarian teaching of Christianity occurred very early, but it was masked by other issues and was not regarded at the time as having the significance which we now see in it. This was the situation in New York City in 1840 when Bishop John J. Hughes of the Roman Catholic Church was attempting to get public funds for the operation of his system of parochial schools. At that time, the New York schools were being operated by a nonsectarian religious group, the Public School Society of the City of New York, which was financed by public funds. Bishop Hughes asked that a portion of the funds be set aside for eight Roman Catholic schools. He based his argument on the ground that the schools then in operation were not religiously neutral and that it would be offensive to Roman Catholic children to have to attend them.[2]

The Bishop cited two major objections to the public schools. First, they read the Bible, but they used the King James version which was a sectarian book. Second, they used books which contained statements prejudicial to Catholics. Thus the easy assumption that the teaching of nonsectarian Christianity was unexceptionable was challenged by a widened pluralism that included religious groups which did not fit under the Protestant umbrella.

The statement that the Bible was a sectarian book must have come as news to the city fathers. Protestants had long assumed that the Bible was the one platform on which they could all unite. And of course they could, so long as they were all Protestants. All Protestants used the King James version of the Bible. But here was a religious group that had its own authorized version of the Bible and its own ideas about how the Bible ought to be used.

Henceforth, any use of the Bible in the schools would be considered controversial.

The accusation of sectarianism in the textbooks must have caused additional dismay. The books were certainly nonsectarian as regards Protestantism. They displayed the stated neutrality of the schools in the area of religion. But they also showed that this neutrality applied only to the claims of competing Protestant sects. Toward Roman Catholicism, their attitude was rather one of bigotry and hostility, contempt and misunderstanding.

The Protestants in this controversy were exasperated by what they regarded as the unwillingness of the Catholics to come to terms. They offered to expunge any offending passages and complained that the Catholics would not sit down with them to help in the process. The Catholics, in turn, argued that they had no assurance that the expunged books would not continue to turn up in unexpurgated form and that anyway the whole system militated against the Catholic faith.

Clearly, what the Catholics really wanted was the help of public funds to continue their system of parochial schools. The complaints about the sectarianism of Bible and textbooks were made in justification of their pleas for school funds. They were not interested in eliminating the sectarian teaching from the public schools, but rather in the support of their own system of schools. There is, however, no indication of bad faith in the stand that Bishop Hughes took. He and most other New York Catholics were convinced that the system was bad for Catholics and that it could not be cured merely by blacking out textbook references to "popery" and "deceitful Catholics."

Since the purpose of the Catholic petition was primarily to obtain funds for parochial schools, the result was simply a widening of the breach between public and parochial schools. There was no movement to discontinue Bible reading or the teaching of religion. The New York City school system was soon brought under the direct control of public authorities, but the content of the teaching was not altered from the pattern that had been instituted in Massachusetts by Horace Mann.

THE SUPREME COURT DECISIONS

Most of the fundamental constitutional issues regarding the place of religion in the schools have been raised only within the past twenty years. The Fourteenth Amendment is now interpreted to mean that the provisions of the First Amendment apply to the states as well as to the federal government. In other words, not only may Congress make no law respecting the establishment of a religion, but the several states are also forbidden to make any such law. Since the schools are regulated by state laws, the whole school question is now thrown into the federal courts for adjudication and this, in practice, means that such questions will ultimately be decided by the United States Supreme Court.

The first major case dealing with church-state separation in the schools was the case of Everson *v*. Board of Education of Ewing Township, which the Supreme Court decided in 1947. The case concerned a New Jersey provision of bus transportation for parochial-school children. The Court, in a five-to-four decision, found that the state could provide such transportation on the ground that it constituted aid to the children rather than aid to the parochial school. In spite of the closeness of the decision, there was no division on the Court as to the requirement for the separation of church and state on the state level. All agreed that the provisions of the Fourteenth Amendment forbid state aid to religion or to religious schools.

Since that time, court cases involving religious issues have been flying thick and fast. A released-time program of religious instruction was declared unconstitutional when it took place in the school building. A similar program was considered constitutional when it took place away from the school grounds. More recently, the question was raised whether or not a prayer, authorized by the New York State Board of Regents, could be used in the schoolroom for corporate worship. In this controversial case, the Court decided that authorization of the prayer constituted the establishment of a religion.

More recent decisions have declared unconstitutional both the recitation of the Lord's Prayer and the devotional reading of the Bible without comment. In both cases the reasoning was the same: such provisions breach the wall of separation that ought to exist between church and state.

The present position of the Supreme Court on the constitutional provisions regarding the place of religion in the schools may be summed up in two very general statements:

1. Public aid to sectarian schools is prohibited, although aid to the children in such schools is permitted if it does not constitute aid to the school itself.

2. Devotional exercises in the schools, including prayers and devotional Bible reading, are prohibited.

The Supreme Court decision on the Regents' Prayer Case met with immediate, widespread disapproval, especially among Protestants, although many Catholics joined in the general condemnation of the Court. The Court was accused of fostering godless education and interfering with practices that had the sanction of custom. The public response to this decision indicated that a large number of Americans still regarded Horace Mann's settlement as being both adequate and right.

There have, however, been extensive changes in the religious composition of the United States since Horace Mann's day. Any impartial examination of the recent Supreme Court decisions, in the light of the realities of contemporary American society, shows that the Court has merely been bringing Mann's settlement up to date. Mann and his contemporaries recognized the need to come to terms with the religious pluralism of the day. It was a pluralism of Protestant sects and the proper response to this pluralism was to work for a nonsectarian Protestant Christian consensus. Today the pluralism is much wider. It includes not only hundreds of varieties of Protestants but also large Catholic and Jewish minorities as well as numbers of agnostics, atheists, and other citizens who can in no way be regarded as self-conscious Protestant Christians.

RELIGION IN THE SECULAR SCHOOLS

In this new context, the nineteenth-century settlement speaks for no consensus. Today anything religious can be offensive and divisive. Anything religious is automatically controversial. In this boader pluralism, even the Bible and prayer itself are sectarian. Thus any genuine neutrality of the school system requires that the school be neutral, not merely as among competing Protestant sects, but neutral as to the validity of religion itself. This new attitude of the public school may be expressed by saying that it has no views about religion. Everyone is entitled to his own views, but he is expected to make his own provisions for worship and teaching. The school will not hinder, but neither will it participate.

Of course this attitude leaves the public school open to the charge of having expelled God, of fostering atheism, and of relegating religion to the periphery of life. Yet no sensitive Christian would require or even expect a child to join in prayers to a God in whom he does not believe. Indeed, who would want his own child to be led in prayer by an unbeliever? Certainly not every teacher is an unbeliever, but some are; and the possibility must be entertained unless religious tests for schoolteachers are instituted, something which the Constitution clearly forbids.

Perhaps we have merely arrived at the logical position of religion in a pluralistic society. Prayer and worship, religious training and nurture are all matters which come under the discipline of home and church. The Supreme Court has removed them from the area of public schooling where, in our society, they have no place. For this the Court deserves the thanks of all faithful Christians and, to their credit, many American Protestants have gradually come to see that this is so.

There is another point in this controversy that is worth mention. The place of nonsectarian religious instruction in the public schools was based on a view of the place of religion in life that is

itself highly suspect. This is the belief that religion is the source
of public morality. The Massachusetts Constitution of 1780
stated this position succinctly when it said, ". . . the happiness
of a people and the good order and preservation of civil government essentially depend on piety, religion and morality." [3]

This outlook was maintained by most conservatives of that
era. As suggested earlier, Benjamin Franklin held this view, as
did John Adams and Alexander Hamilton. The idea is based on
the doctrine that man is so depraved by nature that he will re-
lapse into bestiality unless he is restrained by the forces of law
and order. In order to make the enforcement process easier, man
is given the internal restraints of religion which assure him that
if he gives himself over to his baser instincts, he will suffer dam-
nation. The religious institution is, therefore, to be supported by
all right-thinking citizens, and religion should be taught to the
masses. It is interesting to note that this view is prudential in its
outlook and can be held just as easily by an unbeliever as by a
religious man. Franklin's own skepticism has been noted earlier;
this interest in aiding all religions is not an unusual attitude in a
skeptic.

In our own time, this view of religion is hardly supportable.
Whatever else the increasing secularization of life has meant, it
has not produced a corresponding decline in morality. Certainly
there are signs of moral dislocations in modern life and there is
evidence that the complexity of mass urban society is one of the
factors in increasing crime and divorce rates, to cite only two critical areas. At the same time, it has not been demonstrated that
crime and vice are directly related to religious skepticism. As we
have pointed out, there are numerous agnostics who lead quite
blameless lives just as there are faithful Christians who are mor-
ally less responsible than their unbelieving counterparts. If the
Christian doctrine of man means anything, it means at least that
Christians can make no pretensions to having a higher level of
moral achievement than have non-Christians.

More significantly, Christians challenge any use of religion
that would reduce it to a social function. While religion may, in-

cidently, serve a social function, that is not its purpose. Thus it is a mistake to commend Christianity because it "fights communism," "prevents juvenile delinquency," or "keeps families together." To see religion in these terms is to reduce religion to the status of an instrument, valuable only insofar as it supports other, presumably higher, ends. If religion is to be taught to children because it will make them better citizens, then the end of citizenship has been exalted above the ends of faith.

The Christian would have to counter this view with the assertion that Christianity should be taught only because it is true, not because it serves to make people moral. The proclamation of the gospel has for its end the salvation of man and his enlistment in the service of the Lord. It would be blasphemous to make God's cause serve man's cause.

So Christians cannot accept the teaching of religion as an aid to public order. Yet public order is a good and useful thing to preserve and the ethics of citizenship must be maintained. In this sense, the school is called upon to teach morality. I have already suggested how difficult a task this is because of the inevitable tendency to trespass upon the province of religion. The "democratic values" that the school inculcates can easily become an alternative religion.

While American Christians must remain acutely aware of the dangers and temptations inherent in the teaching of values, they must be willing to run the risk of competition with Americanism-as-religion in order to safeguard the integrity of both church and school. The school must necessarily teach what might be called "the civic virtues," admitting that these are not ultimate values but are rather proximate goals on which Americans can agree as citizens, while continuing to disagree as to the ultimate frame of meaning in which they are rooted. Teachers can be bold enough to suggest that men disagree on why democracy is an appropriate form of government for us; on why men ought to tolerate each other's differences; on the ultimate meaning of life and the goal of history and that, despite these differences men can agree on how they must live together. Men can agree on the need for limited government, the rule of law and personal liberty. They can agree on the demand upon the citizen for fundamental loyalty to his country and on his corresponding right to dissent from the actions and decisions of his government. Men may not all agree that we are children of God, but they can agree that no man may be deprived of his life, liberty, or property without due process of law.

As already suggested, this raises for Americans the problem that they agree on secondary things while differing on fundamentals. They therefore stress the secondary agreements and tend to relegate significant disagreements to the periphery. Admittedly this a serious problem for a pluralistic, democratic society. But the point to make here is that Americans cannot expect their schools to bear the weight of the problem or to provide a solution for it. The school must take the easy way out and limit its teaching to those relative goods to which all subscribe. The school cannot inculcate religion and it cannot be allowed to promote nationalism or democratic values as though they were religious values.

TEACHING RELIGION AS A SUBJECT

If religion is not to be fostered in the public-school program, is there any place at all for religion in the curriculum? It cannot be entirely eliminated. Religion intrudes itself into any serious discussion of man-in-culture. Our own civilization is incomprehensible without some understanding of the religious forces that helped to shape it. In his concurring opinion in the Everson case, Justice Robert H. Jackson made a neat summary of this position:

> . . . it would not seem practical to teach either practice or appreciation of the arts if we are to forbid exposure of youth to any religious influences. Music without sacred music, architecture without the cathedral, or painting without the scriptural themes would be eccentric and incomplete, even from a secular point of view. Yet the inspirational appeal of religion in these guises is often stronger than in forthright

sermon. . . . The fact is that, for good or ill, nearly everything in our culture worth transmitting, everything which gives meaning to life, is saturated with religious influences. . . . One can hardly respect a system of education that would leave the student wholly ignorant of the currents of religious thought that move the world society for a part in which he is being prepared.[4]

Certainly religion is introduced into the curriculum in this sense. It is unavoidable. There is no assurance, however, that it will be handled with detachment, with sympathy, or even with responsibility. The educational system has a long way to go before it will be able to meet these requirements.

But beyond this incidental treatment of religion as it occurs in books, plays, and music, there has been in recent years some appeal by churchmen for more explicit teaching about the part that religion has played in the American past. The subject matter would include the central doctrines of major religious groups, the history that has led them in their separate ways, and the influence they have had on American society.

When it comes to developing programs to achieve this end, however, there has been little agreement. One approach has been the "common core" view that Protestants, Catholics, and Jews ought to get together and formulate propositions to which all can give assent. There are two serious hazards in working out this arrangement. There is, first, the inevitable tendency to water down the content of each group's position, smoothing out the peaks and valleys in order to ensure agreement. The second hazard is more subtle. It is the danger that any "common core" approach would almost inevitably stress the ethical basis of biblical religion. We know now that the basis of biblical religion is not ethics, but the activity of the God who works in history, judging and redeeming, and of his people who are bound to him in covenant. Modern biblical theology has shown us that there is certainly a "common core" of biblical teaching, but it is not yet the basis for consensus among American Christians and Jews.

There is a possibility that religion can be taught in a sane and balanced way. Responsible scholarship can succeed, relatively at least, in being honest about conflict while preserving a sympathetic detachment about the forces that are active in the conflict. In fact, the kind of sensitive, critical treatment of religion that we most need can be provided quite adequately by an unbeliever. All he needs is personal maturity, depth of scholarship, and a willingness to be fair.

There is today, in fact, a considerable movement to develop curricula in religion that will meet both the constitutional and the educational requirements of public education. A number of significant pilot projects have been conducted with encouraging results, showing that, in theory at least, religion can be taught in a pluralistic educational system without creating undue offense.[5]

It is far too soon, however, to maintain that the problem has been solved. Pilot projects and experimental programs are far different from the ordinary routine of public education. They are likely to be well financed, taught by unusually competent and well-trained teachers, administered by people who are convinced of their worth, and generally supported by religious groups and by the community at large. They have, in other words, all the ingredients for success.

But when such programs become built into the structure of public education, they will encounter a whole host of new problems, some of them insurmountable. Even if teachers resist the understandable temptation to gloss over past conflicts in the name of social harmony, there is the opposite danger that the honest facing of old animosities will reopen old wounds and will produce anew bitterness out of historical memory. This is especially likely to be the case in communities which already suffer from intergroup tension. Then too, there is the likelihood that some religious groups will bring pressure to bear on the school to ensure that their point of view gets favorable treatment.

For all of these reasons, it is possible to concede the feasibility of developing sound courses in religion for use in the public schools and yet retain a considerable measure of doubt as to whether or not we are anywhere near the point at which such courses can be generally adopted. Few of our religious groups at present possess the maturity to refrain from interference with any genuinely honest and impartial presentation of the role of religion in American society. Far too few teachers are sufficiently competent to treat such a sensitive and controversial subject in the manner that it requires. Far too few school administrators have either the capacity or the courage to develop such programs imaginatively. Perhaps one small step in this direction could be made by encouraging some universities to develop serious programs in religious studies that would train teachers to perform this important function in time to come. In the meantime, to be sure, let the experimental programs be fruitful and multiply. But in the immediate future it would seem that teaching about religion, as well as religious instruction, will have to be carried on by the churches themselves.

THE CHURCH SCHOOL

The Roman Catholic answer to the question of proper religious instruction has traditionally been to provide a complete alternative school system which includes the specific teaching of Catholic faith and life. Other churches, such as the Lutheran and Episcopal churches, also maintain their own schools in some areas. In some cities, Jews have begun to open their own religious schools based on the Catholic model.

But the parochial school is entering upon a period of crisis. The system groans under the economic weight of competition with the often lavish and expensive public-school facilities: the class buildings, laboratories, athletic fields, and auditoriums. There is an increasing shortage of nuns to do the teaching and Catholic schools have been forced to hire lay teachers whose salaries must approximate those of public-school teachers. Furthermore, with the increasing demand for higher levels of education, Catholic parents frequently feel uneasy about the comparative quality of their parochial schools, since they want to make college possible for their children.

The net result of these pressures has been to increase the agitation for public funds to aid the parochial schools. Catholics argue that their schools are bearing part of the social burden of providing education as a national resource and it is only proper that public funds should aid in the process. They point to the evils of double taxation and claim that the parochial school system relieves the public schools of the responsibility of making room for large numbers of Catholic children. This claim is demonstrably true; it is hard to see how some of the school systems of America's large eastern cities could survive if they were required to provide an education for the great numbers of students now enrolled in Catholic parochial schools.

The courts have, until now, shown little inclination to validate the use of public funds for parochial schools and it seems unlikely that such aid will be permitted in the near future. Aid in the form of textbooks and supplies may survive court tests, but the amounts of such aid will necessarily be too small to provide anything but a stopgap. If the parochial school is to survive with any sort of public help, such help will have to take some other form than direct financial aid.

The suggestion has been made that public aid might take the form of "shared time," a system in which the student could be enrolled in two schools simultaneously. He could take certain "secular" courses in the public school while such sensitive subjects as history, literature, religion, and ethics would be taught by the parochial school. This idea is still too new to have been widely tested, but it seems to hold the promise of a fruitful partnership of church and state in which each institution would retain its own independence and integrity.

Toward the bewildering problems of Catholic education, Protestants ought to adopt an attitude of sympathetic understanding. The old particularistic notion that Catholics who seek public support for their parochial schools are somehow "trying to take over the country" is quite out of place today. Certainly there are valid constitutional objections to public aid for parochial schools but those objections can best be raised and argued by the constitutional lawyers, not by religious bigots. The raising of such issues by Protestant churchmen serves only to convince Catholics that their Protestant neighbors are less concerned with preserving the Constitution than with undermining Catholic education. At present, then, the cause of good will and social harmony will best be served if Protestants admit the Catholic claim that their parochial schools perform a legitimate and useful social function and, therefore, ought to be maintained. Perhaps Protestants would then be able to give some help toward the solution of the problem, rather than merely compounding the difficulties already inherent in the situation.

Protestant church-related schools encounter the same sort of problems as do Catholic schools. Their greatest single problem is the high cost of a good educational program. If the school makes a serious attempt to provide good education, its costs go up so high that it can serve only wealthy constituents who are willing and able to pay the price for ensuring that their children will get into the "right" colleges. Since there is a comparative scarcity of such wealth, it is usually necessary for the school to open its doors to students of all religious persuasions or none, with the result that the religious dimension of the educational program is reduced to a *pro forma* level, limited to compulsory chapel services and required religion courses, neither of which are taken too seriously by the students.

If, on the other hand, the school seriously tries to retain the religious flavor of its educational offerings and at the same time tries to keep the price within reach of church members, it finds that it must make unfortunate compromises with the quality of its educational program. It will very likely cut corners by hiring second-rate teachers and paying them poorly, or it will operate with an inadequate and outmoded physical plant. Its predominant concern for keeping costs down will undermine its educational effectiveness.

There seems to be no middle ground between the church school which offers piety at the expense of sound learning and that which offers a training ground for the sons and daughters of elite families whose socioeconomic pedigrees are more impressive than their theological commitments. Whatever its value as a specialized educational enterprise, the Protestant church school will very likely remain a peripheral phenomenon on the American educational scene.

THE PROTESTANT SUNDAY SCHOOL

The Protestant solution to the problem of religious education has traditionally been the Sunday school. Originating as a means for providing a modicum of general education for poor children who had to work on weekdays, the Sunday school evolved into a method of Christian nurture for the children of church members. At first, the Sunday schools tended to be nondenominational. Today most of them are integrated into the structure of the local church. In some Protestant churches, the Sunday school is larger, more important, and better attended than the church service. Many Sunday schools still maintain classes that range from the Cradle Roll to groups of adults that have retained their corporate existence for a half century.

In spite of this appearance of bustling activity, most perceptive clergymen are skeptical of the possibilities of the Sunday school as a useful structure for Christian education. There has been much experimentation in recent years with the revitalization of its curriculum, but the Sunday school is still not taken very seriously in most churches. While on the national level Christian education maintains a high level of professional competence, on the parish level the record is spotty and, on the whole, not encouraging.

Most churches provide inadequate class time for their Sunday schools. Hardly any church in America regularly provides for more than a single hour of religious instruction each Sunday. Many provide no more than half that. Teachers are normally volunteers who lack training and experience. Class lessons are often thrown together in haste and desperation. Attendance is irregular—on the part of both students and teachers—and little demand is made upon either. Performance standards are almost entirely lacking. The intellectual content of even the best courses is typically very thin. The whole enterprise lacks clear goals and sound methods. Yet the Sunday school continues to creak on, a clanking, rusting piece of machinery that causes embarrassment because no one seems to know quite what to do with it.

Many responsible Christian educators are convinced that if the churches are to develop an adequate educational program, it will have to take the form of a weekday after-school-hours session. Here and there, attempts are already being made to work out such programs and to study their results so that future projects may be built upon their experience. The effort is complicated by the massive time demands made by the public schools, especially in the high schools on the age level where the traditional Sunday school program is weakest. Indeed the public school is in danger of becoming a totalitarian force in the lives of young people, not that it is either undemocratic or dictatorial, but rather that it pervades more and more of the student's life and pre-empts more and more of his total time. A normal school day of eight-to-five is not unusual in many localities. Saturday activities such as band practice, play rehearsals, football and other sports make additional claims on the student's time. Heavy homework assignments keep him busy after school and in the evenings. It is no wonder that, in a situation of such intense preoccupation, the church becomes peripheral and religion becomes a spare-time activity.

The school in America has long been under pressure to expand its activities to embrace every area of life, from child guidance to driver training. Since the great sputnik scare, it has even been under the demand to provide intellectual training. Perhaps it is time for Americans to free their schools from the role of outsize family or secular church. Perhaps American society is now ready to allow the school to cut back its activities and to confine itself to the intellectual task it was designed to perform.

As American affluence increases, more and more families are

able to provide their own facilities for the nonintellectual amenities of life. Nonschool organizations exist in massive numbers to perform such functions. For those families too poor and culturally deprived to provide social, recreational, and cultural activities for themselves, the community might well work toward making such things available through other media than the school system. The growth of recreation departments in many cities and even small towns points to the way in which these aspects of life can be organized on a community level without confusing them with the school's primary function of education.

What we would argue for is not any particular method or theory of education, nor any specific program for community action, but merely to make time available. With a little more time at their disposal, the churches may be able to develop weekday programs of religious instruction that will remove from the schools the pressure to teach religion without violating the Constitution.

The released-time system has this in mind. Released time is a program in which the school excuses children from classes, usually for one hour each week, during which time they attend approved religious education programs offered by churches. A more adequate version of the plan is "dismissed time" in which a period is left on the school schedule for all the children to be dismissed, perhaps an hour earlier than usual. They then attend religious instruction if they so desire. If not, they are free to do anything else. The strength of this system is that it requires little interaction of church and school and consequently little danger of violating the church-state separation principle.

This approach has much to commend it. It involves some difficulty in integrating the religious training into the existing school curriculum but that shortcoming could be overcome. Most significant about "dismissed time" is its acceptance of the secular character of the public school. It also accepts the demand upon the churches to provide their own religious training with their own facilities at their own expense. What is more, it accepts the secular character of American society with its corresponding secularization of the weekend. It admits that Sunday morning is hardly an adequate time for the production of a serious effort at religious education. If the program were widely adopted and made to work, it might even result in a return to a worship-centered Sunday in those churches which are, at present, too rushed and preoccupied by the demands of a schedule that crowds both worship and education into a single busy morning.

But no new system will solve the most serious of the old problems. There is no point in asking the public schools to make available to the churches time to do what the churches are not able or equipped to do. Sunday morning educational programs are admittedly inadequate, but the lack of time is only one factor. The main difficulty is that Sunday school is not taken seriously, either by the children or by their parents. There is no assurance in the "dismissed time" plan that Wednesday's preparation will be any more adequate than Sunday's preparation is now. There is no assurance that teachers of weekday programs will be any more professional than are teachers of Sunday schools.

Then too, the Protestant churches labor under their tradition of pietism and anti-intellectualism. Many Sunday school teachers are fine, wholesome people who have no conception of the basic data of the Christian heritage and many of them are not even slightly interested in the subject. They operate on the supposition that if you love God and love children, that is sufficient. It may have been sufficient in frontier days, but in an age when knowledge is pushing forward on every front, when educational levels are constantly rising, when young people are being exposed to educational programs that are both stimulating and demanding—in such an age, simple-minded, sentimental piety is not only inadequate, it is dangerous. It will lose the allegiance of every thoughtful and sensitive young person who sees through it. If the church is to be engaged in education, it must accept the responsibility to do its work as thoroughly and competently as the secular agency that is doing the same thing.

THE DEMAND FOR EDUCATIONAL COMPETENCE

Many of the proposals that have been put forward to provide religious instruction and training have some merit and deserve a trial. But regardless of the program to be adopted, the churches have first to come to terms with the issue of standards within the context of their own sense of discipline. This means taking education seriously. It means, to begin with, a re-emphasis on the teaching responsibility of the pastor himself. Nearly every church in Christendom recognizes that teaching is an important part of the work of the ordained ministry, but in recent years the average pastor has tended to relegate the teaching task to laymen while becoming himself primarily the director of an organization. The parish church can hardly be expected to function adequately as an instrument for Christian education until the pastor himself is prepared to provide competent leadership.

Taking education seriously also means restoring the intellectual component to church teaching programs. It means adopting genuine professional standards for teachers in the churches' educational programs. It may even mean paying salaries to church-school teachers. This is not such a revolutionary proposal. Churches, after all, pay their clergy. Many of them pay their organist. Some of them even pay their janitors. There is no good reason why they should not consider paying their teachers.

Whether teachers are paid or not, the churches will have to deal with the problem of the training and preparation of teachers. If education is to be made meaningful, both teachers and students will have to be placed under real demands: demands for adequate preparation, attendance and performance. These observations are commonplace. This writer's private view, however, is that not only are we far from this goal, but we are unlikely to move toward it in the near future; the vitality of the churches' educational ministry is in question. Most of the professional people now engaged in helping the churches to understand and perform this task are having similar doubts. This is a critical matter, for the viability of Christian strategy in American society in the foreseeable future rests largely on the dedication and competence of the churches' teaching ministry today.

CONTEMPORARY EDUCATIONAL ISSUES

In the field of public education, the churches are concerned primarily with the place of religion in the educational program since this issue concerns the churches directly and profoundly. But there are a number of other educational issues currently under discussion to which the churches might pay more constructive attention. One of the most significant of these is the question of the proper place of education in a democratic society. The United States is now engaged in a great debate over the quality of its educational efforts. Much of the debate is a reaction to a massive disillusionment with its educational system. Americans have expected great things from education, and it has not produced. There is a nagging suspicion that, perhaps, Americans have been cheated and that blame should be pinned on the guilty parties.

The churches can make some contribution to this conversation through their understanding of the proper function of education. From a theological standpoint, it appears that Americans have exaggerated the role of education and the current disillusionment is at least in part a result of excessive expectations. Education cannot by itself produce the good society. It cannot maintain the highest values of a culture. It cannot take the place of home and church, nor can it combat the effects of mass communication. Education could never fulfill all the various roles assigned to it by different groups within the community. Perhaps the churches can help to transform the educational controversy from a search for scapegoats into an analysis of the proper role and function of the public school in a pluralistic society that still believes in limited government.

Related to the issue of the social role of the public school is the issue of educational theory, usually seen as a debate between the followers of John Dewey and his opponents. In the heat of debate, Dewey himself has become a convenient rallying point for defense or attack, and his educational theories have become either distorted or totally ignored. Actually, hardly anyone who knows anything about education would want to go back to the methods of pre-Dewey days. In this sense, Dewey has won his battle and there is nothing left to fight about. But there is much to fight about when such questions are raised as: How do children learn best? How should children be grouped into classes? What are the relative merits of disciplined versus permissive instruction? Which subjects are essential and which peripheral? Most important of all, perhaps, How should teachers be trained?

Fortunately, the decentralized nature of American education allows for much experimentation in these areas and no exclusive answers need be given. The debate itself is necessary, however, and the churches can make a contribution to it, so long as they do not yield to the temptation to become simply another pressure group with their own special interests. Christianity is not wedded to any specific educational theory and the churches can, therefore, be free to see the issues in their historical and cultural context without imposing the answers before the questions are raised.

In the area of education and social change, the churches have a particular contribution to make. It is indisputable that, in a technological society, education provides the competence which alone guarantees social and economic mobility. This fact is especially important to the poorer classes in society. While one can no longer maintain the illusion that education will solve all social problems, it is nevertheless clear that many of the poor can best be helped by being provided with the educational tools that will enable them to help themselves. If this is to be done, it will require heavy financial expenditures in those areas of greatest need. The poor have neither the political nor the economic power to make available the educational resources which they need. The churches do have this power, or at least they can command it by making clear to their members the moral issues involved. This is one area in which the Christian concern for all of God's children leads simply and directly to a concrete form of social concern and action.

Perhaps the churches can involve themselves in a direct attack on this problem by developing pilot project schools in the inner city, as a disinterested service to the whole community. The school authorities in most large cities are staggering under overwhelming burdens and might welcome even a small attempt at providing help.

In many of the poorer urban areas, classes are crowded, buildings are inadequate, the least qualified teachers and administrators are often forced to grapple with the most serious and perplexing educational problems. Poverty, low morale, cultural deprivation, and poor home support for the educational process all combine to undermine whatever educational effort is being made. Dropouts, unemployment, and delinquency are among the consequences of weak and inadequate educational programs.

Educators are inclined to agree that massive efforts are required to cope with the social dislocations which produce this educational malaise and, in turn, feed upon it. Most municipalities are unwilling to commit adequate resources to the task and would hardly know where to begin if they had all the necessary means. School administrators—not the most daring or inventive species of the bureaucratic genus—are frequently unable or unwilling to break out of old habits and to venture into new territory.

Here is a social need crying out for responsible and dedicated action. Churches could make a real contribution to the solution of this dilemma by opening small experimental schools in strategic areas—something like the recent "head start" project carried on for an adequate number of school years. Such schools could make use of pioneering teaching methods, combined with a sustained attack on the problem of cultural deprivation. Classes could be kept small. Guidance and counseling services could be provided. Children could be exposed to enriching cultural experiences. Children from slum homes could be taught together with children of more affluent urban families. Because of the small size of the enterprise, administrative distractions could be kept to a minimum. The lessons learned from the project could be channeled back to the public schools and the teacher-training institutions.

Churches which engage in such programs would be subject to a number of temptations, to be sure. There is danger in removing a child from his cultural environment without providing him with an adequate substitute. Even worse, perhaps, is the temptation to transform slum dwellers into conventional bourgeoisie without either appreciating the values of their slum culture or subjecting the middle-class alternative to any penetrating criticism.

More important is the fact that any church which accepts the challenge of "pilot project educational endeavor" will have to face the need to commit considerable resources to the effort. There is no point in adding to the already large number of educational institutions operating on flimsy and insecure budgets. The churches should attempt to show what can be done when dedication and vision are supported by adequate means. A multi-million-dollar investment may be required for more than a generation.

Here is a situation in which a genuine educational need exists, a need which everyone recognizes but which has not been adequately met by the community at large. Churches can move in to fill the gap, not just to further the cause of religion, but to provide a much-needed service to the society in which the churches are called to be responsible.

Finally, communities throughout the nation must be aroused to recognize the need to provide adequate resources for education at every level. The churches have a share in the responsibility to awaken the citizens of the land to this need. As educational costs mount, pressure will mount at the same time to cut corners, to shortchange the teachers, to allow facilities to deteriorate, to keep up the façade while letting significant educational effort dwindle. Local churches all over the country have the opportunity to work within their communities to keep education sound and vital. On the one hand, they can keep a careful watch on school boards and officials to make sure that the best possible educational efforts are being made. On the other hand, they can exert their own efforts to shield the schools from irresponsible pressure and malicious interference.

These suggestions are based on the view that, in Christian eyes, education has its own validity as man's attempt to understand the world in which God has placed him. It also serves society in two important ways. First, it provides the technical competence that modern society requires in order to survive. More importantly, it enlists the loyalty of each new generation to the aims and purposes of that society. Christians can affirm and support both of these objectives. While they tend to be suspicious of some of the more enthusiastic proponents of education who see it as the universal solvent for all social problems, Christians accept the fundamental validity of the educational enterprise and can legitimately assist in its struggle for quality and usefulness.

5 THE ELUSIVE QUEST OF THE HIGHER LEARNING

THE FIELD of higher education provides a particularly clear illustration of the process of secularization working its way in an important area of American culture. This has been pointed out by many observers including Richard Hofstadter, who opens his survey of the development of higher education in America with the statement:

There are several major themes that command the attention of the historian of American higher education, but among these the oldest and the longest sustained is the drift toward secularism. . . . There can be no doubt that, while the early American college was founded in an intimate union with the church, modern higher education is predominantly secular.[1]

This chapter will outline the movement from church college to secular university and will catalogue some of the Protestant

100

churches' responses to the movement of secularization. Some observations will then be made about the present state of the university and about the relationship of the church to the university.

Observers frequently illustrate this process of secularization by pointing to the Puritans of Massachusetts, who in 1636 founded Harvard College in order to ensure a fit supply of ministers. The evident piety of that enterprise is contrasted with the present state of higher education in which the chief aim seems to be the training of technicians to maintain the prosperity of a thoroughly secular society. In our time, the state has supplanted the church as the dominant force in higher education. On the modern campus, religion is on the defensive or is totally disregarded.

This summary contains much oversimplification and overstatement. Moreover, as Professor Hofstadter demonstrates, it is not entirely accurate as a description of the movement of American higher education. Protestants, appealing to the myth of Protestant America of the past, tend to exaggerate the decline in the church's influence in education by exaggerating its original influence.

Harvard, for example, was indeed established by Puritans in order to ensure the colony of a supply of fit persons to serve as ministers, but the colony was also concerned about the general state of learning. Harvard was a creature of the established church, but it was also a creature of the colony. As historian Frederick Rudolph points out, the General Court of Massachusetts provided financial support to Harvard well beyond the end of the colonial period. The Court also exercised control functions which included closing the college down completely at one point.[2]

These early colleges were deeply conscious of the fact that they were serving a public function. In the colonial era of the state church, however, there was no collision between the religious function and the public function. All of the colonial colleges were religious in some sense and maintained some church ties. Even the University of Pennsylvania, which was founded independently of any single religious group, had an Anglican priest as its provost at the time of the Revolution.

THE ERA OF THE DENOMINATIONAL COLLEGE

While the Revolutionary period brought to an end the easy state-church alliance that had characterized the colonial period, it did not end the church's influence in higher education. For a time, it was debatable as to just where the function of higher education would fall: within the province of the church or that of the state. There was some attempt on the part of state governments to secularize the colleges, but most of those early attempts failed. William and Mary College, for example, elected to retain its ties with the Episcopal Church rather than to become subject to the Commonwealth of Virginia. The most famous controversy of this period in higher education was the Dartmouth College case in which the State of New Hampshire tried to replace the president and board of trustees, transforming the college into a public institution. Daniel Webster's eloquence before the Supreme Court ("It is . . . a small college, and yet there are those that love it . . .") saved the college as a private foundation. But Chief Justice John Marshall's decision took the view that a chartered college was a private corporation that could not be controlled by the state. As a result, the state college movement was set back nearly a half century.[3]

The Dartmouth College decision opened the door to an era of free enterprise and unlimited competition in the field of private college-founding. The "middle period" of American history is characterized by the growing strength and aggressive competitiveness of the Protestant churches. The religious skepticism that had been fashionable in the post-Revolutionary period declined both in the colleges and in society at large. Protestant churches became the leading founders of colleges in the period up to the Civil War. From 1800 to around 1860, the "denominational college" was the typical form of higher education in America.

Many of the colleges founded during this period were located in the frontier areas of western New York and Pennsylvania, Kentucky, Ohio, Indiana, and Illinois. The motives for their founding were varied and often thoroughly mixed. There was the concern of the churches in the East to combat the primitivism and irreligion that seemed to characterize the frontier. There was the understandable concern of each religious group to keep its members faithful to the denominational tradition. There was, too, a less justifiable desire to outdo the other denominations. The competition between denominations was supplemented by a corresponding competition between towns for the location of colleges. Every town with any pretensions to future growth felt the need for a college to demonstrate that it had a future. The result of these competitive drives was a proliferation of colleges, most of them very small, very poor, and very weak.

The weakness of the colleges was partly a result of the manner of their founding. Typically, the process began when some enthusiast would decide that a specific area simply must have a Congregationalist (Presbyterian, Methodist, etc.) college and would journey back East to raise money. If he were lucky enough to get two towns bidding for the college, he might receive some local support: a gift of land or money. A building would be erected as soon as a sum of money was available. Usually the money was inadequate and the building would be mortgaged from the start. The initial support seldom carried the project further than this point. As time went on, other projects would compete for funds and the original supporters would lose interest. The president would have to resort to repeated trips back East to beg for money, with varying success.

Colleges, consequently, tended to be shoestring operations. They could easily be destroyed by the first calamity that was encountered: a fire, an epidemic, a business depression, or internal dissension. Since the colleges were usually creatures of outside enthusiasms and were oriented to serving the needs of the denomination rather than those of the community, they enjoyed little support from the people among whom they existed. With such a collection of obstacles to overcome, it is no wonder that so many of them failed. By the time of the Civil War, a total of 104 colleges survived in sixteen states. In those same states, a total of 412 had already failed, a mortality rate of over 80 per cent.[4]

Most of the surviving colleges just barely continued to exist. Their teachers were usually clergymen, often men who had failed in the pastoral ministry. Much of the teaching was done by tutors, recent graduates who had not yet decided upon their life's work and who remained at the college for only a short time.[5] Neither professors nor tutors received special training. Their meager salary payments were often far in arrears. Student bodies were small, most colleges finding it hard to keep enough students to stay alive. As a result, colleges often operated preparatory schools, and the two types of students tended to be mixed with one another. It is difficult, in fact, to distinguish the college from the prep school in this era.

The financial picture of the surviving colleges does not indicate any great degree of affluence. Hofstadter reports for the year 1840 that 173 colleges shared a total of 16,000 students, an average of 93 students per college. Sylvanus Duvall's study of Methodist colleges reveals that, in the year 1856, total resources per student amounted to $172.00, counting land, buildings, and other facilities.[6]

It would be a mistake to see the church college of this era as a mere creature of the denomination. As we have suggested, most of the colleges were founded by individuals, an interested clergyman or a philanthropic layman. Often the moving spirit in the enterprise, if a clergyman, would become the first president. No matter how loyal a churchman he might be, the college was his child and he would do battle for it, even against the church itself. The tension between church and college might take the form of the college's assertion of independence. More often, it was over the college's battle for funds.

None of the churches assumed any major share of financial responsibility for the maintenance of their colleges. The only advantage of church affiliation for the college was the privilege of appealing to congregations for funds. Being related to a church, therefore, was no guarantee that a college would continue to exist. On the other hand, it was clear that without a church connection, a college had little chance at all. Very few colleges founded in the pre-Civil War era were able to survive without church support. Even most of the state-supported colleges fell upon evil days.

The place of religion in the life of the denominational college varied widely. Its flavor varied widely too, from the broadly Christian outlook of the older colleges to the narrow sectarian exclusiveness of some of the smaller denominational schools. Religion normally permeated the life of the college at all levels. Indeed, church colleges were more interested in promoting piety than in encouraging learning. Though few colleges maintained religious tests for either students or faculty, it was assumed that the college had the duty of fostering Christian attitudes and practices.

The practice of religion took many forms. Compulsory morning and evening prayers were common and Sunday religious services were universal. Extracurricular devotional and missionary societies flourished and withered in their turn. There was usually an annual day of prayer; revivals took place with clockwork spontaneity. The curriculum naturally included courses in Christian evidences and moral philosophy, though there was little emphasis on Bible courses. These would come later as an outgrowth of literary and historical studies of the Bible.

Thus religion occupied an important place in the total life of the church college, though its contribution was not always creative or constructive. It is significant for an understanding of the age to realize that religion held a similar place in the nonchurch college. At midpoint in the nineteenth century, nonsectarian religion was established in the colleges just as it was in the public-school system of Horace Mann's Massachusetts.

The pre-Civil War college retained the traditional classical curriculum that went back to the Renaissance. Greek and Latin language and literature formed its basis, along with mathematics, logic, and moral philosophy. Some enlightened colleges offered elementary physics and a few offered astronomy. On the whole, it was hardly the sort of fare to attract the nineteenth-century farm boy into the classroom.

There was continued pressure for the liberalizing of the curriculum, but little was done about it. In 1828, Yale University met the issue head-on with a faculty report which defended the traditional curriculum as an appropriate intellectual discipline. The Yale Report held that the classical curriculum was essential to the practical man who, presumably, could get his practical education elsewhere. With the powerful authority of Yale behind it, the Report became a model for the liberal arts college in subsequent years.[7]

The result of this commitment to an outmoded and irrelevant curriculum was what might be expected. The colleges became almost completely estranged from American life. The nation was entering an era of unparalleled development in its economic life, in industry and in technology. There was a need for sound, practical, scientific education based on a democratic selection of students. But the colleges refused to heed the demands of society. They insisted, in the name of their Christian heritage, on providing an education suited to a leisured aristocracy but quite out of touch with the realities of American life. The colleges were sure that they knew what was best for students, but the students responded by avoiding the colleges in ever increasing numbers. With so many opportunities offering themselves to energetic and intelligent young men, who would want to shut himself up for four years in an ivory tower?

Since students were so hard to get, colleges were forced to buy them. Tuition was incredibly low. Self-help programs enabled students to work their way through college. Some colleges owned farms and grew their own food. Low faculty salaries kept budgets at minimum figures while contributions were sought to cover the persistent deficits. Students for the ministry were usually given reduced rates or were admitted free. Still the colleges did not grow. By 1850, the more perceptive leaders of higher education were beginning to admit that perhaps something ought to be done to change the situation. As the Rev. Francis Wayland, President of Brown University, put it:

We have produced an article for which the demand is diminishing. We sell it at less than cost, and the deficiency is made up by charity. We give it away and still the demand diminishes. Is it not time to inquire whether we cannot furnish an article for which the demand will be, at least, somewhat more remunerative? [8]

THE RISE OF THE SECULAR UNIVERSITY

The Civil War marks a watershed in American higher education for, at the close of that war, there came of age two related movements that together were to transform the face of American academic life. The first of these was the state college movement, which received a massive stimulus in the Morrill Land Grant College Act of 1862. The second was the university movement which sought to pattern American higher education on the German model rather than on the traditional English model.

The Morrill Act provided grants of federal land, or its equivalent, to all states for the establishment of public colleges for the study of agriculture, mining, and mechanics. The act attracted little public attention at first, but it soon proved a welcome benefactor to public higher education of a practical sort. It ensured that every state would have at least one technologically oriented educational foundation in the public domain. Some of the older states used the land grant to strengthen existing institutions, while other states founded new colleges. The funds available under the act were not large, but they provided a needed stimulus for the raising of other funds and for the acceptance of public responsibility for higher education.

The university movement found a welcome home in some of the new state colleges and infiltrated the private colleges as well. One reason for its rapid spread was its immediate success. Cornell University, for example, combined the resources of the New York land grant with the private benevolence of Ezra Cornell and the vision of President Andrew D. White to produce a university dedicated to a wide concept of learning and useful knowledge. Cornell was ready to teach anything that students wanted to study and the students responded by enrolling in large numbers. Here, obviously, was the answer to Dr. Wayland. The university would receive support from society when it began to address itself to the felt needs of that society.

This new concept of the university can best be seen in Johns Hopkins, which was founded in conscious imitation of the German model. Hopkins was conceived as a center for research and specialization. At first, it had neither undergraduates nor dormitories. Its customary mode of instruction was the seminar which was devoted to the meticulous analysis of source materials and the reporting of research findings. Students were expected to maintain a high level of achievement in their own research.

The contrast between the new university and the old college was striking. The Yale Report of 1828 had been based on the assumption that the purpose of a college is the preservation and transmission of a fixed tradition of learning. The new university assumed the possibility of an indefinite expanse of knowledge and consequently defined its goal as that of discovery. Hence the collegiate emphasis on the classics was replaced by an emphasis on science. The university's radical openness to the future proved to be in accord with the prevailing tendencies of American life.

The university brought with it a new attitude toward the student. The college had stood *in loco parentis* to the student because it was concerned with the production of a certain kind of person. It therefore regulated the student's private life with more or less strictness. It prescribed the hours he had to keep. It regulated his drinking habits, his social behavior, his personal morals. The university, to the contrary, was concerned only to train the mind. The student was to be allowed to live his own life. This early freedom of the student was soon eclipsed by the general mores of American society. It probably reached its high-water mark with the elective system introduced at Harvard by President Charles W. Eliot, a system in which the student was permitted to take any course he wanted, with no requirements stipulated by the university.

At the same time, the college faculty was developing, for the first time, a professional character. The university insisted on special preparation for the college teacher. He was expected to have done advanced study in his area of specialization. He was expected to pursue his own research. The Ph.D. degree was instituted, though it would be many a year before most college teachers were to attain to that degree. Faculty salaries rose, and the prestige of the college teacher increased accordingly.

The twin movements of public higher education and the secular university continued to expand until, in our time, they combine to dominate the scene in American higher education. While the eminent old private universities continue to exist, most of them today receive massive amounts of public money, usually in the form of research grants. Whether public or private, the university still places a high value on those aspects of higher education that appealed to the original supporters of the university movement: the pursuit of truth as a primary goal of higher education; an emphasis on research and publication rather than classroom teaching; a concern to serve the needs of a technological society; and a high standard of professional competence in the faculty.

At the same time, the university has undergone a process of Americanization that would make it unrecognizable to an inhabitant of the nineteenth-century German institution after which it was modeled. Whatever its status, undergraduate education continues to be an important feature of every university in America. Even Johns Hopkins University found it expedient to establish an undergraduate college. With the undergraduate have come dormitories, advisers, extracurricular activities, and above all, football. The university of America today is something of a compromise between the traditional "English college" and the modern "German university."

One feature of the university that has remained constant is its secular character. From the very first, the university has been a threat to the church college. President Eliot of Harvard summed up the scorn felt for the denominational college by the new breed of academicians when he noted, "A university cannot be built upon a sect." [9] In view of the excessive conservatism and intergroup rivalries that characterized the church colleges of the early nineteenth century, Eliot certainly had a point. It is doubtful whether any American church could have guaranteed the freedom required for the unfettered pursuit of truth wherever it might lead. The overwhelming success of the secular university called for a response from the church colleges, and their ability to make an adequate response was in doubt.

THE CHURCH COLLEGE IN A SECULAR AGE

The responses of church colleges to the new academic climate varied widely. They ranged from the repudiation by some colleges of their church connection to the conservatism of others who fought a rearguard battle against the university in the name of the Yale Report and traditional values. As time went on and the university movement grew and prospered, the church colleges were placed in an ambivalent position. Because of their denominational ties, the parent churches expected that they would continue to serve as training grounds for the youth of the denomination. At the same time, the increasing heterogeneity of the religious population required a de-emphasis of denominational particularism to ensure a continuation of funds and students. The church tie itself became something of a drag where it had once been a support. It cut the college off from possible sources of income, especially from the new "captains of industry" who were more interested in the practical education offered by the universities than in the classical education traditional in the church colleges. If the college were to have a free hand in changing its curriculum to meet the new conditions, the restraining hold of the denomination would have to be loosened or broken.

The older and stronger colleges led the way. It is significant that today none of the original colonial colleges retains its religious ties, except as a quaint survival. It was only natural that those colleges which had built up large endowments and institutional prestige should be most inclined toward independence from the church. The new leaders of business and industry who now dominated their boards of trustees were not impressed with the need for a church connection. An added impetus to the divorce of college from church was the work of the private philanthropic foundations which began around the turn of this century. The Carnegie Foundation, for example, made large grants toward the establishment of pension programs for college faculty but specifically excluded denominational colleges from participation. As Dr. Rudolph observes:

Foundation influence was strong . . . and more than one denominational college threw off its denominational connections in the hope that its new-won freedom could be exchanged with Mr. Carnegie's standardizers for a pension program. Bowdoin, Wesleyan, Rochester, Drake, Coe, Hanover and Occidental were among the institutions that found their denominational connections, obviously hitherto tenuous, now dispensable.[10]

The remaining church colleges muddled through the first half of this century with their future rather clouded. The end of World War II, however, brought the G.I. Bill of Rights and an accompanying glut of students to all American campuses. As that wave of students receded, higher education continued to be sustained by an ever increasing number of college enrollments. Since 1946, nearly every college in America has participated in the greatest seller's market that higher education has ever known. The college boom assured the immediate future of the church college and revivified many a dying college that ought, perhaps, to have been allowed to expire.

At the same time, a revival of religious interest throughout the nation has strengthened the church ties of most church-related colleges. Not many of them are leaving the ecclesiastical fold today. There are numerous forces in contemporary higher education, however, which make the future of the church college problematical. Questions have been raised as to the quality of the church colleges and the need for their continued existence.

A recent study of 295 Protestant church colleges compares them with 87 other colleges which, though once church-related, now identify themselves as private colleges. Comparing such factors as accreditation and the presence of Phi Beta Kappa chapters, this study ranks the nonchurch colleges noticeably higher.[11] A more recent study, conducted by the Danforth Foundation, makes much the same judgment, but qualifies it with the observation that there is a very wide variation in church colleges, many of them ranking among the best of the private colleges while others linger near the bottom of the lists.[12]

Most of the criticisms of church colleges made in the Danforth report center around the lack of any sense of distinctive purpose. Church colleges tend to imitate other colleges, and their models, more often than not, are the secular institutions. As a result, the church colleges share in the prevailing tendency of most American higher education to concentrate on day-to-day responsibilities to the neglect of larger issues such as educational philosophy, curriculum design, and the distinctive role of the specific institution. This neglect shows itself in the haphazard selection of faculty and students, the fragmentation of the curriculum, and the absence of any clear set of institutional priorities.[13]

Curiously, the role of religion in the church college is especially ambiguous and superficial. In the absence of a carefully-thought-out view of the nature of the church-college relationship, the college frequently regards the parent church merely as a source of financial support which must be kept mollified but is not to be allowed to participate meaningfully in the academic process. Thus religion is most honored on the level of official outward observance. A certain number of ministers sit on the board of trustees. Rules forbidding drinking are enforced on campus. College publicity materials contain carefully guarded statements about the distinctive role that religion plays in campus life.

Usually, there is a college chaplain, though he is often harried and overworked with teaching and administrative duties. Since he serves at the pleasure of the president, he has no real independence, no leverage with which to develop a genuinely prophetic ministry. Compulsory chapel has disappeared from most college campuses, but chapel services remain. They are often devoid of any specific theological or liturgical content, relying heavily on home-made forms of worship, "inspirational messages," and "dynamic guest speakers." Established campus religion, therefore, is likely to produce only contempt for the whole religious enterprise, especially among the more sensitive and gifted students and faculty.

The classroom teaching of religion has improved remarkably in this generation. The increasing number of superior students taking advanced degrees in theology and religion at major universities may be one reason for the increase of competence among college teachers of religion. The contemporary professor of religion is no longer likely to be a superannuated clergyman, a returning missionary, or a refugee from the parish ministry.

Many church colleges still require courses in religion of all students. For the most part, religion courses center around the historical and literary study of the Bible. Surprisingly few church colleges offer adequate majors in religion or religious studies, though the practice is increasing. Still more rare is the presence of serious interdisciplinary programs which relate the insights of theology to literature, history, sociology, or the arts.

The effect of the religious program in the church college is hard to measure. The Danforth report concludes that the amount of religious knowledge among graduates of church colleges tends to be significantly higher than among graduates of public or other nonchurch institutions. But there is a wide range among the church colleges themselves, with students of Roman Catholic and conservative Protestant institutions ranking significantly higher in this sample than those from liberal Protestant institutions.[14] It would seem fair to say that the teaching of religion at church colleges is not without effect, though the possibilities have not really been developed in any significant way.

The financial situation of the church college has always been somewhat precarious. Today, with few exceptions, church colleges are still pinched for money. To be sure, their financial position has improved noticeably in the past twenty years.[15] New buildings have risen; endowments have been augmented; faculty salaries have increased. But the financial future of the church college is still unsettled.

The whole of higher education faces a continuing economic crisis, with budgets and tuition skyrocketing from year to year. Massive state aid and supplementary federal funds can be expected to solve the cost problem for most public colleges and universities. The church colleges, barred from access to such funds, can hardly expect to compete. Private benefactions tend to go to the already rich and prestigious institutions. As a result, the gap between affluence and poverty in higher education is likely to grow. Already tuition at church colleges is two to five times higher than at public institutions, though frequently the latter are academically superior.

If the church college is to provide quality education within the framework of its own distinctive purpose, it will require from the church the same kind of financial support which the states give to their best colleges and universities. Few churches have ever given their colleges this kind of support. Given the excessively large number of church colleges now in existence, it is doubtful whether any of them will ever be able to do so.

Perhaps the first step in providing adequate church support to higher education would be to reduce the number of church colleges. Drastic as such a step would be, it may not prove to be as harsh a measure as it sounds. With the present continuing demand for higher education throughout the nation, it may not be necessary to close any colleges at all. Some could be merged, with the physical facilities of the weaker institution being offered without charge to the appropriate public higher-education authority. Other institutions might be transferred by agreement to public authorities to be administered as state colleges. This might prove particularly feasible in states which are now desperately trying to expand and upgrade public higher education. It might even be possible to maintain some form of Christian ministry on those campuses by retaining a chapel as church property or by developing a religious ministry outside the institutional framework of the college, in a manner appropriate to a public institution.

No doubt such a step would require a genuine spirit of sacrifice on the part of a religious institution noted more for the preaching of sacrificial giving than for its practice. The sacrifice would be greater in the realm of institutional pride and nostalgia than in concrete reality. The movement would constitute a shortening of battle lines in the interest of greater strength and concentration. Overextended commitments have already led to the loss of many church colleges and to the deterioration of quality in many others. The loss of specific institutions with time-honored church ties would be more than adequately balanced in the long run by the added vigor and competence of those that remain.

Any such move would, of course, be quite ineffective unless it were coupled with a decision on the part of the churches to support the remaining church colleges on a level comparable to the support enjoyed by state institutions. This would require a financial commitment substantially larger than that which any church now provides.

A more fundamental question arises at this point: Why should the churches be willing to provide this kind of financial support to their colleges? What justification is there for the traditional connection between college and church?

Vast claims are often made for the church college. Guy E. Snavely, former Executive Director of the Association of American Colleges, maintains that "the church and the four-year college have been the chief agencies responsible for the rapid rise of the United States to its prominence as a world power." [16] Most apologies for the church college are somewhat less pretentious. They usually cite the small size of the institution, its concern for the individual student and its greater emphasis on the humanities. When these claims are analyzed, however, they betray considerable confusion as to just what is being defended. The distinctions claimed for the church college are shared by the small nonchurch liberal-arts college as well. On the other hand, they are less obviously shared by large urban church-related universities.

Professor W. O. Doescher, for many years a teacher in a Lutheran college, has made the more modest assertion that the church college alone can produce a genuinely Christian culture because it believes in God:

The justification of the denominational college . . . resolves itself to this: It takes the fact of God and his redemptive action in history so seriously that it is willing *to assume the responsibility of treating it as an objective fact* that can be commended to the young mind before that mind is able to evaluate it critically.[17]

This claim is to be taken more seriously. What does it mean to say that a college "believes in God?" How can Christian faith be validly enshrined in an academic institution? How can it be manifested? How can it be continuously maintained? Any claim of the church college to a distinctive role in American higher education today will be evaluated on the basis of its ability to respond to this sort of question.

The Danforth Foundation report has already been cited as calling attention to the comparative weakness of church colleges in their sense of institutional purpose. The same report goes on to make a number of recommendations for the revitalization of this sense of purpose. It encourages the church college to develop an experimental attitude toward its own life and work and suggests the development of pilot projects that have significance not only for the sake of the college itself but for the sake of higher education as a whole.[18]

The report suggests that the church college take advantage of its small size to make good its claim that it has a unique concern for the individual student. American Protestantism has often been excessively individualistic, but in an age in which students are frequently reduced to the status of faceless statistics in many large educational enterprises, the affirmation of a sense of individual worth may provide a needed counterweight.[19] Hopefully, that concern would take a more sophisticated form than the old-fashioned, moralistic *in loco parentis* attitude.

The commitment to the individual student calls for a corresponding dedication to the task of teaching. By and large, church colleges do not expect their professors to engage in research. At the same time, few have made any sustained attempt to recruit, retain, and reward superior teachers. Church colleges are in a position to demonstrate real leadership in this area. They could, moreover, begin to develop long-range experimental programs for the training of new college teachers, one of the most glaring inadequacies in contemporary higher education.[20]

The Danforth report also recommends that church colleges settle on the humanities and public affairs as their main academic emphases.[21] The emphasis on public affairs has not been strong in the past, though it is surely justifiable on the ground of the church's interest in developing a socially aware and responsible laity. The interest in the humanities is of long standing, but may be expected to take new forms.

In the past, the church college's choice of the humanities was often tied in with a rejection of science and anything else that seemed practical. Church colleges still tend to accept and foster the two-culture dichotomy that C. P. Snow has called upon us to repudiate. They oppose the forces of religion to modern science in the name of an ideology that is hostile and suspicious of the modern world.

The church can ill afford to have this negative attitude toward science and technology take root in its institutions of higher education. In our time, the churches ought to be in the forefront of the movement to relate science and technology to the genuine needs of society. This can be done only in an atmosphere that affirms the legitimate goals of the scientific enterprise.

A commitment to the humanities need not carry with it this antiscientific bias. Indeed, science itself ought to be taught as one of the humanities. In modern higher education, the humanities cannot be understood merely as what goes on in departments of Philosophy, Literature, Religion, and the Fine Arts. Humanistic study is a way of looking at any subject in its ultimate dimensions, in the light of its implications for the life of man and the meaning of his existence. It is in this sense that the church college ought to be committed to the humanities.

But these project suggestions, legitimate though they may be, still do not answer the question of the church college's distinctive mission. This mission has to do with relating the insights of Christian faith to the academic discipline. Somehow, church colleges must find ways to clarify this purpose and to implement it in the life of the institution. The Danforth report recommends that every church college think through and publish a statement of its purpose for its own guidance and the guidance of all who may seek to study or teach within its walls. It calls for a core group of faculty and administrators who are committed Christians and who consciously accept the purposes of the institution. Certainly this proposal raises questions in the area of academic freedom, but the problems involved may not be insoluble. As the report states:

The chief obstacle to accomplishing this reconciliation (of freedom, responsibility and institutional purpose) is the tendency of many people to absolutize commitment and absolutize freedom, thus making them mutually exclusive in an educational setting. But wise administrators and mature teachers know how to avoid this pitfall.[22]

It will be clear from the foregoing discussion that church colleges exist today in the midst of great difficulties and greater anxieties. It is likewise clear that they face the future with some doubt and hesitancy. Many educators and even many Christian laymen are convinced that the church college has outlived its usefulness and ought to be abandoned. The churches have too many demands placed on their inadequate resources already. There is no point in tying up vast sums in higher education, a field in which other private and public agencies have shown themselves responsible and competent. In this view the church college is not worth preserving because it is doomed to play only a minor role in American higher education in future years.

It is true that the church college is, and will continue to be, a minor force on the educational scene. At the same time, there is no need for it to settle into an academic backwater. The pluralistic character of American higher education opens up to the church college the possibility of making a unique contribution both to higher education and to the church. In order to fulfill this function, the college will have to be provided with adequate resources and dedicated leadership. There is no assurance that either will be forthcoming, but signs are already appearing that make the situation seem hopeful.

THE CHURCH'S MINISTRY IN THE SECULAR UNIVERSITY

The vast changes in higher education in the mid-nineteenth century produced a new phenomenon in American culture: the secular university. Its private forms and its public forms were largely indistinguishable except for their tuition charges. In either case, the traditional alliance with the church was shattered and religion was excluded from the university either by law or by custom. While it took some time for these new tendencies to make themselves felt, by the end of the century the secular university displayed an attitude that was, if not hostile, at least indifferent to religion.

Much of the hostility can be attributed to the reaction of the early university reformers against the narrowness and petty spirit that characterized the church colleges of their day. The open and liberal climate of the secular campus contrasted favorably with the cramped authoritarianism of the church college. The new universities rapidly filled with young men and women who were in outright rebellion against organized religion and against orthodoxy, whether religious or academic.

The initial response of the Protestant community was fear and concern. The Christian educators fought the secular university every step of the way. As the university won its way despite the opposition of the churches, the latter strove to find ways to fight the secularism that the university produced.

The first agency to do religious work on the state university campus was the YMCA which began its ministry at the University of Michigan in 1858. The "Y" sponsored prayer meetings and promoted interest in missionary activities. Inspired by the early successes of the YMCA, the churches soon began to enter the field of campus ministry. The Episcopal Church started its work on the Michigan campus in 1886 and the Presbyterian Church followed in 1887. Both churches provided chaplains and developed denominational student centers.[23] In other places, local pastors made special attempts to reach college students and to form special groups for them within the congregation. The development of the denominational campus ministry ran up against considerable opposition from the church colleges which were disposed to point out that, if all good church members were in the church colleges where they belonged, the expensive and overlapping student ministry in the state universities would be unnecessary.[24]

In 1904, the Presbyterian General Assembly recommended the appointment of special ministers to Presbyterian students in state universities. They were to provide religious and biblical instruction as well as pastoral supervision—what we would call counseling. Lutherans and Episcopalians relied more on the ministry of the local church, leaving most of their campus work to the parish clergy.[25]

In either case, the campus pastor was seen as exercising a caretaking function. He was expected to get acquainted with the students of his denomination and to take care of their spiritual needs. He was expected to do what he could to combat the atheism of the classroom. He was also expected to recruit candidates for the ministry. His program provided a full community life within the circle of the denominational fellowship. The agency for this purpose was the "Foundation," whose name originated in the ambitious proposals for the raising of large endowment funds to support the campus ministry. The money seldom materialized, but the name stuck. The Foundation usually had a building which resembled an ecclesiastical fraternity house, with a kitchen, meeting rooms, and recreation areas. Its program embraced ping-pong, parties, and pastoral relations.

Denominational campus ministries coexisted with the YMCA, now often called the Student Christian Association, since it included both men and women. The relationship was not without its tensions. From the "Y" viewpoint, the denominations were invading its preserve, bringing with them sectarian rivalries and narrow concerns where there had previously been only friendly co-operation and a broad general appeal. Actually, most campus pastors maintained a healthy ecumenical spirit. Having been thrown together, they normally worked together. They shared in joint activities such as the Student Volunteer Movement and the later Student Christian Movement. Indeed, the campus ministry moved ahead of the mainstream of American Protestantism in its ecumenical concern and activity.

On their part, the denominational pastors criticized the "Y" for its theological vacuity, a charge that was hard to deny. The attempt to be all things to all men did contribute to a genuine loss of any Christian distinctiveness. And it was likewise true, as the churches pointed out, that the "Y" abstracted the student from participation in the ongoing life of the church. It acted as a denomination itself, but it embraced only the college years. After graduation, the "Y"-oriented student was left with no place to go and, consequently, he often drifted out of the life of the church altogether.

On the other hand, the "Y" pioneered in many areas of campus life. It involved students in settlement houses, summer camps, and social work, giving vast numbers of middle-class students their first real look at urban poverty—and many of them never forgot the experience. It initiated a ministry to foreign students. It developed the first student personnel services in many universities: counseling, placement services, student loan funds, student centers with lounges and recreation facilities. As time went on, the university took over most of these ventures and incorporated them into the official student program. Still, it is the "Y" that deserves the credit for leading the way.

Throughout the twentieth century, the Protestant campus ministry has been growing in numbers, in vitality, in stature, and in finances. A great spurt of activity occurred in the 1950's with the increase of student population and the revival of interest in religion. By that time, however, the aims and methods of campus ministry were coming under considerable criticism. Most of this criticism came from the campus ministers themselves.

The campus pastors were concerned primarily with the inadequacy of their own conception of student work. They felt themselves restricted to denominational enclaves composed exclusively of undergraduates, especially freshmen and sophomores. They felt out of touch with upperclassmen, graduate and professional students, faculty and administration members. Incoming students would get involved in their programs but, with time, they would go off to other interests. Gradually the pastors came to the conclusion that campus religion was becoming a spare-time activity that competed for the student's time and attention with other and more pressing concerns.

The full-scale Foundation program provided a church-centered community life that paralleled that of the university itself, but the university did most things better. The college dances and fraternity parties were more exciting than anything the religious organizations could provide. The demands of the classroom were more exacting than those of the chaplain's study groups. Most students found that they did not live, eat, or study only with other members of their denomination and consequently most of them saw no reason why church membership should determine the shape of their campus life.

So it happened that the religious club and the denominational

Foundation tended more and more to recruit the academic misfit, the social outcast, the withdrawn, and the uncomfortable. The group gravitated to the fringe of campus life and became least attractive to those students who were most involved in the central processes of higher education. The campus pastor spent most of his time counseling and otherwise dealing with the problems of disturbed students.

As the campus clergy became aware of this situation, they began to think and work their way out of it. The process of change has begun only recently and it still lacks consistency or coherency. So far, it has produced a fundamental shift in the campus minister's attitude toward the university. The older version of campus pastor was likely to look with some suspicion upon the university, seeing it primarily as a housing development to be exploited for the sake of the church. Today the campus pastor is more likely to affirm the central purpose of the university. He probably will tell his students that their first job on the campus is to be students, preferably good ones. He sees the church's task as a ministry within the university, not in opposition to it.

Then too, the modern college minister is beginning to accept the logic of secularization. No longer is he likely to demand the use of college facilities or to expect to have a privileged place on the calendar for his programs. He is likely to de-emphasize social programs, not because they are evil or frivolous, but because he expects students to provide their own entertainment. Students are thus free to develop their own social life without feeling any obligation to attend the Presbyterian party or the Methodist mixer. At the same time, the campus Christian community is free to fulfill its central functions: corporate worship, the preaching of the Word, the ministration of the sacraments, and the correlation of Christian faith with the academic disciplines and the concerns of higher education. This version of campus ministry is based on the conviction that the vocation of the Christian in the university is to work out for himself, and with others, the meaning of responsible Christian witness in a secular society.

As a part of this reappraisal of function, the campus ministry has enlarged the scope of its task to include the graduate student, the faculty member, the college administrator. The campus pastor therefore needs an acute awareness of the fundamental issues of higher education and a sensitivity to the social dynamics of a university. One by-product of this new conception of campus ministry is the encouragement of a longer tenure for the pastor, since there is increasing need for men with long experience on the campus. The genial young clergyman with a crew-cut and a ukulele is no longer adequate to the task.

The recent past has also seen a broadening and deepening of the ecumenical thrust of the campus ministry. Very little in a campus religious program is necessarily limited to a single denomination. Communion services and church membership classes are about the only exclusive activities. Social service and action wear no denominational labels. Study programs, whether they deal with the meaning of life, higher education, politics, or theology are even more effective if they include participants from various religious traditions.

An increasing awareness of the fragmented character of university life has led many campus ministry staffs to develop team ministries, parceling out various areas of the campus to individual staff members. Thus the Presbyterian may be assigned to work with graduate students, the Methodist to undergraduates, the Episcopalian to the faculty, the Baptist to the medical school, and so on. This arrangement enables the staff to cover some segments of the campus in depth, while each pastor has a chance to make use of his special gifts and interests. Thus it is more than a gesture in the direction of public relations that has dictated a general change in title. Whereas a campus pastor was once designated as "Chaplain to Episcopal Students at ——— University," now he is called "Episcopal Chaplain to ——— University."

The contemporary campus pastor sees his role to be that of engaging in theological dialogue with his entire campus, or that portion of it which constitutes his special responsibility. He retains the traditional function of nurture: worship services, counseling, teaching, and contacting new students. But at the same time, he seeks to bring into existence a community of theologically perceptive persons who understand something of what Christians believe about God's saving activity in the world.

THE TEACHING OF RELIGION IN THE SECULAR UNIVERSITY

The question of teaching religion in a secular university is separable from the question of the church's ministry in the university, but it is not unrelated. Secular universities still harbor a deep-seated dread of becoming involved in the disputes of warring religious factions. Public universities are legitimately sensitive about preserving the integrity of church-state separation. Thus the place of religion in the academic curriculum is still controversial.

Many thoughtful observers maintain that all academic subjects should be permeated with a theological viewpoint and that therefore no need exists for a department of religion in a university. This sounds rather like the old theology-queen-of-the-sciences point of view, although this is not what most modern Christians intend. They mean that there is a significant theological dimension to the study of history or politics or economics. But even this view oversimplifies the issue. What we want to maintain is that the Christian faith has implications for all of these areas. The implications arise out of the discipline but they are not an inescapable part of it. There is, for example, no such thing as "Christian economics." Economics operates according to its own inherent logic and if the Christian wants to understand that logic, he must go to the economist, not to the theologian. Yet economic issues raise theological questions and to deal with these questions, it is necessary to relate the insights of the theologian to the insights of the economist.

The logic of academic life would seem to require, therefore, the study of religion as a separate and distinct discipline. This is obviously true in the case of comparative religion, but that is not where the controversy comes in. The question is, rather, whether it is possible to teach Christian theology, Bible, church history and Christian ethics as academic subjects. I believe that it is not only possible but that it is necessary.

Christians may object that this procedure would put religion into a single watertight compartment. The answer, of course, is that there is no need for the compartment to be watertight. The influence of Christian faith in all areas of life does not mean that Christianity cannot be studied in itself. All academic subjects interact with one another in various ways. Science has significant implications for modern society, but elementary physics does not take up these implications. They must be dealt with, to be sure, but first there is a need for people who know a great deal about science and people who know a great deal about society. The same can be said for religion and any other subject matter. The interaction of religion with other subject matter is a phenomenon that takes place in persons, not in disciplines.

But how can a person teach religion in an academic setting? Is not faith in Christ something different from information about him? Certainly this is so, but the academic task is limited to providing information. It is not the task of the classroom to seek conversion of the student. Faith is a gift of the Holy Spirit, not of the university. Granted it is difficult to teach theology with detachment, but it is difficult to teach any subject with objectivity when one really cares about the matter. Impartial teaching does not mean that the teacher is indifferent to the material. It means that he is honest about his own views and is fair in his presentation of other views. This is by no means an easy task, but it is not essentially different for the teacher of religion and the teacher of politics. There are teachers who perform this feat every day. It is no less than the task of the good teacher.

The teaching of religion on the college level is a requirement for any educational program that seeks to understand the meaning of Western civilization. More and more universities are recognizing this fact and are developing religion courses. For the most part, these courses are academically respectable and are staffed by teachers whose competence is indisputable. As they win their way on the campus and make a contribution to the total academic program without bringing about ecclesiastical intrusions, they will help all universities to see that religion has a rightful place in higher education. If the question of religion in the curriculum is seen in this way, it will be understood as a contribution to education and not to Christian faith. This is the only ground on which the teaching of religion in a secular university can be justified.

When the case for religion is made on educational grounds, it becomes apparent that there is no good reason why religion cannot be taught in the public colleges and universities. The barriers to such teaching are psychological and sociological, not theological or constitutional. Some denominations might object that their point of view does not receive a fair hearing. Others might object that the teaching is slanted, partial, or overcritical. If this happens, the university administrator will justifiably prefer to wash his hands of the whole business. Educators are deeply sensitive to the bitter and vicious squabbling that has been characteristic of American religious groups. They are even more sensitive to the threat of ecclesiastical pressure and control in the academic process. Certainly the history of higher education in America offers good ground for their fears.

If religion is to find a place in the curriculum of the public college and university, it will have to be brought about without undue pressure or interference from the churches. All churches will have to accept the fact that, when the story of Christianity is told, either historically or theologically, their own contribution is going to come under critical scrutiny, if it is not completely ignored. If the churches are willing to take that risk, the universities may be willing to take seriously their responsibility to provide an opportunity to study this controversial but significant aspect of Western culture.

CHURCH AND SECULAR UNIVERSITY TODAY

The attempt of the churches to develop a ministry within the secular university has provided the occasion for a fruitful dialogue concerning the nature of the university itself and the church's relationship to it. The conversation has been going on for at least two decades. The British sociologist and theologian Arnold S. Nash, writing in 1943, criticized the academic pluralism of the contemporary university. Referring to the tendency of each discipline to absolutize its own methodology and conclusions, he pointed out, "The liberal democratic university, by rejecting any real attempt to discover and then teach a unified conception of life, refuses to be a university." [26]

More recent observers have maintained that the university needs a belief in "an ultimate value in human life." One such critic has pointed out: "What higher education must seek more earnestly for itself and for its students is that quality added to knowledge which results in wisdom and appears as the product of a balanced development." [27]

The question of values is one which, admittedly, the modern university has been loath to face. The scientific method has been adequate to produce a revolution in the shape of society, but it has been of little use when the question concerns the ends of society or the problem that man presents to himself. Those questions have received far too little attention in the modern university.

Professor Nash's solution to the problem was to admit the theological dimension once more into the dialogue within the university. He proposed to do it in a certain way.

Christian churches need a fellowship of lay theologians or Christian scholars who would view it as a part of their vocation as a Christian intelligentsia to create a Christian world view within which the conclusions of the specialized subjects of the University curriculum could be given their ultimate meaning in terms of a specifically Christian philosophy of man and his relations to the historical process.[28]

The trouble with this solution is that it seeks, implicitly, to reverse the process of secularization by turning back the clock to the era of Christendom. The state of knowledge today is such that no agency, much less the church, could sell any unified conception of knowledge to the academic world. For the church to make such a proposal would smack of the ecclesiastical domination associated with the Middle Ages. The most likely result would be the end of whatever communication the church has been able to establish with the academic community.

If the church is to make any contribution to the "university question" it must first accept the facts of life. The first fact of modern university life is the fact of secularization. The university is free of the church. Both church and university are—or can be—better off because of the separation. It is now possible, for the first time in Western history, to propose a genuine dialogue between church and university, a dialogue in which the terms are not imposed, because both parties are free. The task of the church is not to provide ready answers to the questions of the university but, rather, to see that those questions are raised and humbly to contribute to the search for the answers. The time is ripe, then, for a new beginning in the relationship of Protestantism and higher education.

As the churches have come to terms with the fact of secularization in the university, they have begun to see the positive values in this type of higher education which encourages diversity, openness, and the free espousal of various positions, commitments, and points of view. Similarly, as the churches have begun to abandon their negative attitudes toward the university, the universities themselves have grown less fearful and suspicious of ecclesiastical encroachments. The rabid anticlericalism of the early days of the university movement has been replaced by an attitude toward religion that, while not without its skeptical side, is more inclined to be appreciative and even sympathetic.

It might be pointed out that, just as the late eighteenth century saw the separation of church and state, so the late nineteenth century saw the separation of church and university. The latter separation was anguished and painful. It provoked hostilities that lasted long after the break. Indeed, the break is not complete even today. But in the meantime, both institutions have made some adjustment to the new situation and there is now the possibility that they can begin to relate to each other as free and co-ordinate, in a relationship based on mutual confidence and respect. Church and university have their separate roles to play in American culture and yet they share many areas of mutual interest which they would do well to explore together.

This point is an important one, for a serious lack of open and honest communication still exists between church and university. When one reads the church-produced literature on "the university question" one is struck by the feeling that the theologians conceive of the university as an inert object which can be examined and evaluated by a living "community of faith." Yet the university is just as alive and responsive to evaluation as the church. If there is to be fruitful dialogue and interaction between church and university, it will have to be based on the understanding that dialogue is a two-way street and that both institutions have much to learn from each other.

The possibility of useful co-operation of church and university may be increased as these two institutions begin to realize how similar they are and how similar is their position in American society. Almost all the criticisms customarily leveled against American Protestantism could be applied with equal force to the American university. Just as the variety of American Protestantism makes its description difficult, so the observer of American higher education would have to single out diversity as its most obvious feature. Institutions of higher learning differ remarkably in size, physical surroundings, intellectual level, social climate, affluence, complexity, educational philosophy, attitude toward students, and almost any other feature that could be mentioned.

Both church and university in America share the opportunities and temptations that arise from their extraordinarily close relationship to American society. Both have suffered in their history from the charge that they have been irrelevant to the genuine needs of that society. Both have responded by making society's demands their first order of business. Consequently, both have tended to become subservient to the society, to the detriment of their proper tasks. Critics of the American churches frequently call attention to the instrumental character of American religion. The same criticism has been made of American universities. Professor Nash has pointed out that the modern view of higher education "tends to degenerate into the notion that the universities are service stations for the convenience of a democracy that makes ease its god." [29] More recently, Richard Hofstadter has made the similar point that American society has faith in the uses of education without having a comparable understanding of the cultural content of education.[30]

Yet there is in Protestant Christianity and higher education a built-in counteracting influence. Both church and university have traditionally seen a part of their social role to be the criticism of existing society. It is this critical function that is most endangered by the excessive readiness to serve society on its own terms. The rejuvenation and exercise of this critical function will do much toward saving both church and university from complete domination by the secular forces represented by the militant commercial spirit of American culture.

While both church and university are committed to the spirit of honest soul-searching and creative self-criticism, no social institution can properly criticize itself without some outside help. Criticism is a duty that dedicated men owe to one another. The most promising aspect of the new mutual openness of church and university is that each might benefit from criticism by the other.

At the same time, since both church and university labor under pressures emanating from society at large, each could profit by receiving encouragement from the other in support of its independence. Too often, churchmen add their voices to the hysterical clamor that calls on the university to perform feats beyond its capacity or to perform services that are detrimental to its main concerns. The demand on state universities to accept every high school graduate, for example, has frequently contributed to a serious debilitation of higher education. Similarly, the persecution of teachers or students who hold unpopular views, while no longer common, is not yet a thing of the past. In situations such as these, in which the society at large exerts pressure on the university to betray its own integrity, the churches could well offer it their disinterested support.

This dual task of mutual support and criticism might be the special ministry of that large and growing group of people who are, at the same time, members of both church and university, whether as students, teachers, or administrators. They could conceivably provide the advance guard who could begin the task of interpreting the church to the university and the university to the church. In particular, this task will devolve upon those men who are placed within the context of the university but whose primary institutional loyalty is to the church: namely, the campus clergy. While this ministry retains the functions which have already been described, there is no doubt that campus pastors occupy a unique strategic position in contemporary life. They are given the paradoxical task of working within a major social institution on the basis of a set of insights and commitments that come with them from a different dimension of knowledge and concern.

Space does not permit any detailed treatment of the many specific problems that beset the contemporary American university. Suffice it to say that any such list would have to include the problem that the availability of funds too often determines the focus and direction of research and educational endeavor. It would have to include a host of similar perplexities: the conflicts between the demands of teaching and those of research; the inadequacy of all present methods of evaluating college teachers and most methods of evaluating students as well; the breakdown of communication between academic disciplines; the loss of the personal dimension in college teaching; the tragic alienation of the student in the large, urbanized university; and, not least, the problem of financing higher education without starving out the marginal private institution or bankrupting the public purse.

All these issues have their theological dimension which the churches would do well to state. All of them involve psychological, social, economic, political, and educational issues which make it impossible for the theologian or anyone else to dogmatize about their solution. As massive and complex social issues, they will have to be dealt with through many approaches, taken patiently and cautiously, by men who are deeply concerned for higher education for its own sake and for the sake of the society which it serves. The churches have no monopoly on this kind of concern, but they certainly ought to share the concern and they ought to share in the conversations that are directed to dealing with the problems.

America has come a long way from the time, only a century ago, when the ecclesiastical institution dominated the field of higher education. The churches proved then that they had no special capabilities that would enable them to operate colleges. The modern university, which has since come into its heritage of freedom, has benefited from that freedom. Now that the churches can admit that this is so, perhaps the church and the university can once more dare to enter into dialogue with each other.

6 THE DEVELOPMENT OF A PROTESTANT SOCIAL CONSCIENCE

THE PERIOD following the Civil War brought significant changes into American life. While the nation's attention was focused on the issues of war and slavery, the American economy passed what Walt W. Rostow has called "the take-off point." According to Rostow's analysis, this is the point at which an economy has acquired sufficient capital, transportation, power and technological resources to make possible a decisive break with the traditional past. The next stage of growth, the "drive to maturity," is characterized by the continued build-up of large industrial enterprises dominated by hard-driving managers. It is also likely to involve serious dislocations in the society because of the rapidity and the unevenness of the forces of change.[1]

The American drive to maturity occupied most of the latter half of the nineteenth century. That era saw the creation of giant corporations and trusts that served to concentrate wealth in the hands of a few powerful men. The new masters of American economic life were rapacious and extravagant. Their excesses gave the names for the era: "the gilded age"; "the great barbecue."

If America's economic growth exacted its toll, the price was paid by another class of people. The other side of the coin of prosperity was the misery and squalor of the city slums. The wealth of the "captains of industry" was matched by the abject poverty of the privates in the industrial army.

Industrialization meant the growth of large factories which required a large labor force. The concentration of a large laboring population led to a phenomenal growth in the size and complexity of industrial cities. Thus the two revolutionary forces, industrialization and urbanization, sustained and fed on each other. Between them, they transformed the face of America.

The resulting social revolution posed a major challenge to the Protestant churches. Previously, their attention had been directed to meeting the challenge of the frontier. Protestantism had conquered the frontier by means of the camp meeting, the revival, and the circuit rider. In the process, however, Protestantism had itself been conquered. It had acquired a rural flavor that made it uncomfortable in the rising cities. It had taken on a middle-class tone that made it uncomfortable in the midst of the laboring class. In spite of these handicaps, Protestantism took on the challenge of the factory and the city. It cannot be said that Protestantism triumphed, but it was radically altered by the encounter.

This chapter and Chapter 7 will discuss the urban-industrial challenge and the Protestant response. Chapter 7 will deal with the many ways in which the Protestant churches reshaped their ministry so that they could function in the industrial city. This chapter will be concerned with the corresponding movement within Protestantism to understand and to reshape the new social and economic forces themselves.

This latter movement has been called "the social gospel." The term is not wholly satisfactory, since it has been used to describe everything from moderate social reform to radical Christian socialism. Yet there is probably no other expression that serves so well as an over-all, blanket description of the entire movement.

In church circles, the social gospel has fallen into some disrepute in recent years, though it may be due for rehabilitation. At present, the very idea of social reform still arouses suspicion among the religious. Reformers are customarily pictured as naïve do-gooders, compulsive busybodies, or anxious people who are running away from their own problems. No doubt there is some truth to the accusations, but the evils which the reformers fought against were real. We can afford to regard them lightly today only because the reformers were so effective in combating them.

The social gospel has been accused of theological superficiality. Its doctrine of man was excessively optimistic, its view of history progressive, its idea of God immanentist. The social gospel intruded economics into religion and substituted social analysis for the Christian faith. It turned the church into a social service agency instead of a community of faith in Jesus Christ. Again, these charges may have some validity. When we examine the historical context of the social gospel, however, we can only conclude that it was a deeply religious and socially responsible attempt of convinced Christians to do the work of the Lord in their world.

What was the social gospel? What did it do? It was an attempt to apply the insights of the Christian faith to the contemporary social scene. It produced a massive shift in American Protestantism, a shift from an exclusive emphasis on individual piety and morality to a concern for social and economic reform. To understand the significance of this shift, let us look briefly at the social attitudes of American Protestantism before the social gospel did its work.

PROTESTANT SOCIAL ATTITUDES IN THE GILDED AGE

Conservative critics of the social gospel frequently claim that it substituted economic doctrines for Christian teaching. Yet the individualistic Protestantism of an earlier day had its own concern for economic doctrine. Indeed, the prevailing economic orthodoxy was understood as universal, inexorable, unchangeable divine law. Textbooks in political economy were customarily written by clergymen and were couched in theological language.

Among the accepted economic doctrines was the wage-fund theory which assumed that there was, in the economy, a fixed total amount available for the payment of wages. Consequently, if wages rose in one area, they would have to be lowered in some other area, or there would be unemployment. This theory explained why employers could not possibly raise wages even though they might wish to, for to do so would violate the divine laws governing the economy. Trade unions, of course, were an unmitigated evil since they disregarded the laws of nature and worked against the true interests of their members.[2]

Along with the wage-fund theory went the view that labor was a marketable commodity, strictly subject to the laws of the market place. This conclusion was accepted uncritically by most churchmen. Moreover, since the laws of supply and demand regulate the wages of labor and since these laws are divine and unchangeable, it follows that poverty is inevitable and that charity, except for the sick, is a violation of natural law which can produce only disaster. Even those who called for the exercise of Christian charity tended to look upon the poor as existing only to be the objects of their charity. As one religious periodical noted: "The poor we have with us always; and this is not the greatest of our hardships, but the choicest of our blessings. If there is anything that a Christian may feel thankful for, it is the privilege of lifting a little of the load of some of his heavily burdened neighbors."[3]

It is not hard to see why the churches were losing contact with the working classes during this period. For the most part, churchmen were convinced that any man of energy and good intentions could work his way out of his working-class status. They could explain the middle-class composition of most churches by pointing out that the virtues of the churchgoers caused them to rise in the social scale. The Protestant message to the working class was simply, "Work hard, obey your masters, and put your money aside so that you can own your own business someday." The complete unrealism of this advice did not occur to them because few churchmen—especially the ministers—had any first-hand knowledge of workingmen or their problems. It never occurred to them that a man might work hard all his life without ever having any money to lay aside for the future. Nor did they appreciate the significance of the changes then under way that were producing, for the first time in America, a permanent working class, a self-conscious proletariat, who could not look forward to any change in station during their own lifetime. The typical Protestant, minister or layman, was simply out of touch with this whole side of American society.

The general complacency of the American middle class that followed the victories of the Civil War was not seriously challenged until the economic reverses of the 1870's produced a period of labor unrest. The climax came in 1877 when the railroads decreed a 10 per cent wage cut. All of the railroad workers east of the Mississippi went out on strike and a series of bloody fights and riots broke out. Troops were called out to suppress the strikers, and strikebreakers were brought in to take over their jobs. From that time until the end of the century, the labor question was the central focus of Protestant social concern. The struggles of capital and labor provided the issue out of which the social gospel emerged.

In its response to the railway strikes of 1877, Protestantism disclosed its social outlook. It identified with the leadership of the business community, even in its inconsistencies. The economic doctrine of *laissez-faire* was generally accepted by Protestants. It meant that the government could not interfere with business because the economy had to be allowed to develop according to its own natural laws. But the free action of the market place did not extend to the operations of labor unions. It was the duty of government to defend property by opposing the efforts of strikers—dispersing their pickets and breaking up their public gatherings. When troops were called out to quell rioters, the churches were unhesitatingly, even hysterically, on the side of Law and Order. An editorial in the *Congregationalist* shrieked:

> Bring on the troops—the armed police—in overwhelming numbers. Bring out the gatling guns. Let there be no fooling with blank cartridges. But let the mob know, everywhere, that for it to stand one moment after it has been ordered by proper authority to disperse, will be to be shot down in its tracks. . . . A little of the vigor of the first Napoleon is the thing we now need.[4]

Even in liberal theological circles, the attitude toward the strikers was little different. In discussing the issues behind the strikes of 1877, the Rev. Henry Ward Beecher, popular preacher, exponent of the New Theology and one of the highest paid clergymen in the United States, denied that the wage cut was adequate cause for a strike. Said Dr. Beecher, "It is said that a dollar a day is not enough for a wife and five or six children. No, not if the man smokes or drinks beer. . . . But is not a dollar a day enough to buy bread with? Water costs nothing; and a man who cannot live on bread is not fit to live." [5]

To a sensitive contemporary reader, these remarks sound incredibly callous, especially since they come from the leading religious spokesmen of the day. But these men were not personally hard or cruel. They were the victims of an outmoded and unworkable social and economic theory. Because of those theories, they were effectively insulated from the actualities of the industrial world of their own time. They did not see the problems and they could not understand the issues from the point of view of the working class. It is small wonder that they were able to develop so little social conscience.

THE EARLY SOCIAL GOSPEL MOVEMENT

Nevertheless, the social conscience was already in process of development. Indeed, in limited ways the development had been going on for some time. Leading scholars of the period have pointed out that feelings of sympathy toward labor had been quietly growing since the Civil War. As yet, these tentative stirrings were isolated and ineffectual. The climate of the age was one of complacency and optimism. It was not until the dislocations of the 1870's that advanced social thought could get a hearing. But with the strikes and riots of 1877, the new movement came to the surface and rapidly gained ground.

The best-known leader of the early social gospel movement was the Rev. Washington Gladden, minister of the First Congregational Church of Columbus, Ohio. Primarily a moralist, Gladden was not especially profound in his social analysis. Nevertheless, he had some direct experience with labor troubles in Columbus and he was able to see some justice in the workers' cause. While he did not condone strikes, he recognized their necessity. Contrary to general Protestant opinion, he accepted the labor union as a legitimate agency for the redress of employees' grievances.

Gladden was a simple, honest, and plain-spoken man. It is perhaps because of his transparent sincerity that he won for himself a hearing in every important social group. He was a prominent preacher and he wrote a number of books which brought his views to the attention of churchmen throughout the land. While he frequently addressed groups of businessmen, he was popular with workingmen's groups as well. His most important public statement, an address entitled "Is It Peace or War?" was first delivered in 1886 to an audience composed of union men. He later gave the same talk to a gathering of substantial businessmen. In it, he defended the rights of labor, recognizing that in labor as in politics, war might sometimes be the lesser of two evils.

The cure for industrial warfare, Gladden believed, was the application of Christian love to labor relations. If all men could unite as brothers under the fatherhood of God, industrial peace would ensue. In the realm of practical reform, he recommended the introduction of profit-sharing systems and reduction of the hours in the working day. In later years, he advocated factory inspection, the regulation of monopolies, and the regulation of the hours of work. His greatest contribution was his simple recognition of the bargaining rights of labor, a recognition that most Protestants were unwilling to make. Otherwise, his major achievement was to serve as a focal point for the new movement. A source of inspiration for a whole generation of followers, he was the means whereby a collection of new ideas was introduced into a church that was increasingly ready and willing to receive them.[6]

The chief impetus for the early social gospel movement was the impact of economic depression and labor unrest. The first important Protestant response was a dawning realization that labor had some justice in its cause. As sensitive men like Gladden and others came to see and appreciate the condition of working-men, they were willing to commit economic heresy in the name of Christian morality. Yet since they lacked a theoretical basis for their social views, their analysis tended to be superficial and their remedies either inadequate or utopian. A fresh perspective was offered by the Christian socialist movement then active in England, while a new theoretical critique of American economic ideas was offered by the German historical school of economics.

British Christian Socialism was never a very powerful movement, but it did much to awaken the social conscience of the Church of England. Since it regarded itself as the national conscience, the Church of England felt some sense of responsibility for all levels of British society. Churchmen such as Frederick Denison Maurice and Charles Kingsley presented a Christian critique of capitalism on moral and religious grounds, with just a touch of antibourgeois romanticism. Their movement for education, cultural opportunity, and the return of craftsmanship, grounded as it was in the old high Tory tradition, contained little promise for the long-run future. Its contribution to the American churches was the idea that economic institutions could be brought to the bar of Christian judgment. The Episcopal Church, probably because of its close relationship with the

Church of England, was especially infused with radical social views. Among the radicals were Dr. R. Heber Newton, Father J. O. S. Huntingdon, William D. P. Bliss and Bishops Frederick Dan Huntingdon and Henry C. Potter.

More scientific in its outlook and also more promising for the future was the economic theory imported from Germany during the last decades of the century. Throughout the nineteenth century, American scholars had been going to Germany to obtain the kind of higher education not then available in the United States. By the 1880's, the movement of returning scholars was beginning to bear fruit with the establishment of the new universities. At the same time, entire schools of traditional thought were being supplanted by new ideas, many of them German in origin.

The first break with traditional American economic views came in the work of Francis A. Walker, who would hardly be classed as a progressive by contemporary standards. Yet Walker repudiated the idea that economic theory is based on divine laws and he rejected the wage-fund theory which had been the basis for much conservative economic thought.

The leading spokesman for the new economics was Richard T. Ely, who has been described by Professor Henry May as "one of the most important single influences on Christian social thought." [7] Ely was a German-trained economist whose exposure to the German historical school of economics led him to criticize not only the wage-fund theory but the concept of *laissez-faire* itself. He saw no excuse for the government to sit idly by while men suffered and starved. In his critical studies of socialism, Ely was dispassionate and fair. He was sympathetic with the struggles of the labor movement and called it "the strongest force outside the Christian Church making for the practical recognition of human brotherhood." [8]

Ely appealed to the churches for social concern and responsibility. More clearly than most theologians, he formulated the social nature of Christianity. He repudiated the excessive otherworldliness of the churches and called the simple gospel of Christ "a one-sided half-Gospel." He called for "a social as well as an individual gospel" that would include provision for the salvation of society.[9]

In addition to his scholarly work, Ely also participated actively in a number of religious and professional organizations that furthered social gospel teaching. He spoke to church groups, lectured at Chautauqua, wrote on social and religious questions, and rallied others to the social gospel cause. He consistently called for training in the social sciences as a part of the professional equipment of the clergyman. Partly as a result of his urging, courses in social ethics were instituted in a number of seminaries long before the discipline of sociology was introduced at many universities.

One of Ely's major contributions was the founding of the American Economic Association in 1885. Although its first president was the more conservative General Francis A. Walker, Ely was the moving spirit behind the enterprise. It was not founded as a social gospel organization, but it included a large number of Protestant clergy who, like Ely, were seeking a scientific understanding of society as a basis for their ideas of social reform.

CONSERVATIVES, RADICALS, PROGRESSIVES

By the 1880's the complacency of earlier decades had been pretty well shattered by labor strife and the attention of the churches was turned increasingly to the problems of labor and capital. It is possible to distinguish, by this time, varying strands of response to the industrial crisis. Professor May, for example, describes a conservative and a radical school of Christian social thought. He sees a moderately progressive party between the other two and he restricts the use of the term "social gospel" to this broad, central group. His restriction is justified by the fact that this latter strand of Christian social thought has proved most enduring and influential.[10]

Though conservatives still tended to oppose unions, many of them were willing to admit that all was not well on the labor front and that there was an increasing danger of the rise of a virulent socialist movement. For that reason, conservatives were willing to discuss such reform measures as people's banks, cooperatives, and the like. On the whole, however, they preferred to rely on the willingness of Christian employers to pay higher wages and to ameliorate the lot of the workers voluntarily.

The radicals, though never more than a small minority in the movement, enjoyed an influence far beyond their numbers. On the one hand, they could blaze the trails that other thinkers might follow later. On the other hand, they made the middle-of-the-road progressives seem more conservative to the church at large and, hence, more acceptable.

One of the most colorful of the radicals was the Episcopal priest, William Dwight Porter Bliss of Boston. In 1889, he organized a Society of Christian Socialists to build a bridge between the church and the growing socialist movement. He edited (and wrote most of) the movement's own newspaper, *Dawn*. He participated in a wide range of social gospel organizations, including the Church Association for the Advancement of the Interests of Labor (CAIL) and the Christian Social Union, both unofficial organizations in the Episcopal Church. He edited the *Encyclopedia of Social Reform*. From 1890 to 1896, he founded and ministered to the Mission of the Carpenter, a Christian Socialist congregation in Boston.

Bliss had the optimism of the radical and confidently anticipated the future development of socialism without violence or catastrophe. Thus, while he looked for the eventual "development of the Christian State," he was yet willing to devote himself to the piecemeal reforms characteristic of the period.[11] He believed that the most important work of the socialist in the meantime was to educate the people so that they would be led to desire that which was best for them.

The Christian Socialist position was also upheld by George D. Herron, a fiery midwestern preacher who was one of the most controversial clergymen of his day. A chair of Applied Christianity was founded especially for him at Iowa College, now Grinnell. Herron can be called a socialist only because he opposed the capitalistic system of private property. He had no clear views about the kind of social order that ought to replace it. He believed in the necessity for self-sacrifice and for the conversion of the whole society. He called for common ownership of land and he advocated industrial democracy in the realm of production. He espoused the cause of political socialism, though he had little faith in the schemes of unregenerate men. His version of the social gospel has been called "a deeply religious interpretation of the contemporary social revolt, phrased by a prophetic genius of tremendous spiritual dynamic." [12]

Herron was a major influence during the years 1893 to 1901. He was a great preacher in the revivalist tradition. Thousands came to hear his sermons and lectures. He traveled from Boston to San Francisco on speaking tours, producing controversy wherever he went. By 1898, his radical views caused him to resign his professorship. In 1901, a scandal erupted when he divorced his wife and immediately married the daughter of his benefactress. From that time on, Herron was isolated from the church. What little influence he had was limited to the Socialist party.

There were other Christian radicals, of course, with their own organizations, newspapers, and magazines. But on the whole, Christian socialism was a small movement with little lasting influence, either in the church or in the secular socialist movement. Nevertheless it served as a gadfly to many who were not likely to espouse such radical causes themselves, but who still wanted to work for the reform of American society.

It is the moderate social gospel tradition that is most important in the long run. By the 1890's, it was becoming a major force in American Protestantism. The proponents of social Christianity could be listed by the thousands and the list would include many important names. While the movement seems to have got its start in the Congregational, Unitarian, and Episcopal churches —notably those churches which shared the establishmentarian concern for their whole society—by the turn of the century it had spread to nearly every major denomination. Organizations grew up and special projects developed out of the social passion.

Josiah Strong, whom we have already met as an advocate of American overseas expansion, was a leading figure in the social gospel movement of the 1890's. A Congregationalist minister, Strong had served as secretary of the American Home Missionary Society in Ohio. In 1885, he published a remarkable book, *Our Country,* in which he summed up the problems and the opportunities for the Christian mission in the America of his day. The book was an instantaneous success and made Strong into a church leader of national prominence. Soon he was called to become executive secretary of the Evangelical Alliance, an interdenominational organization which, for some years, had been sponsoring conferences for the discussion of contemporary social problems.

Strong revitalized the Evangelical Alliance and, during the next seven years, promoted three significant conferences at which the social dimension of the Christian faith was explored. The first conference, held in Washington, met on a note of crisis to explore areas in which the church was not responding to its missionary call. The topics included the city, the family, capital and labor, immigration and the misuse of wealth. The second conference, more optimistic in tone, dealt with methods of expanded church work. The third conference, which met during the Chicago World's Fair of 1893, was concerned with the social task of the church and ways of accomplishing it.[13]

The chief contribution of the conferences was to bring together the leading exponents of social Christianity and to assure them that they were not isolated from the mainstream of the church. At the same time, the prestige of many of the participants and the sheer size of the events made them newsworthy and attracted the attention of newspapers and magazines. By this means, the message of social Christianity was carried back to the churches. By the turn of the century, nearly every Protestant body was aware that among their number were those who believed that Christianity involves one in concern for the life of society and that social, economic, and political issues are relevant to the Christian faith.

The process of spreading the social gospel through the churches was facilitated by another medium, the popular novel. The best known of these was *In His Steps: What Would Jesus Do?* by Charles Sheldon, a Kansas clergyman. It tells the story of a town in which the minister proposed that everyone attempt to decide each question of their lives by asking, "What would Jesus do?" and then doing just that. The proposal was adopted by a number of parishioners—a phenomenon which justifies classifying the book as fantasy—and the entire city was thereby transformed. Sheldon's work enjoyed an incredible popular success, first as a serial in a denominational publication and then as a book which was reprinted endlessly in various languages.

In His Steps was only the most popular of a large number of similar books, most of them pious and sentimental and hardly worth attention as serious fiction. Their solutions to social problems were artificial and naïve. Yet they served to point out, often with accuracy and passion, the serious dislocations of American society. They called for the application of Christian moral fervor to the righting of social wrongs. They dealt with political corruption, crime, prostitution, liquor, the moneyed interests, labor problems, and evil business practices. They opened the eyes of many respectable churchgoing middle-class American Protestants to the vast unsolved problems of modern industrial society and thereby helped to turn Protestant attention to social concern and reform.

THE SOCIAL GOSPEL INSTITUTIONALIZED

As the new century dawned, the social gospel movement became an established part of American Protestantism. In the first decades of the twentieth century, it found both institutional expression and theological formulation.

The earlier period of the movement was characterized by a multitude of organizations, both denominational and interdenominational, devoted to the spread of social Christianity. After 1900, the churches began to adopt the social gospel officially. At the instigation of the Church Association for the Advancement of the Interests of Labor, the Episcopal Church instituted a Commission of Capital and Labor in 1901. In 1913, it was made permanent and was given a full-time field secretary. The National Council of the Congregational Churches appointed a similar commission, also in 1901, and employed its first full-time staff member in 1910. The Presbyterian Church established a Department of Church and Labor in its Board of Home Missions and called a full-time secretary in 1903. By 1914, nearly twenty Protestant churches had some kind of board or commission devoted to social problems.[14]

In 1908, these interests coalesced in the founding of the Federal Council of Churches of Christ in America. This organization was the first official multidenominational effort in American history, representing the culmination of a movement of interchurch co-operation that extends back to the beginning of the nineteenth century. Other organizations, such as the Evangelical Alliance and the Institutional Church League had been interdenominational in character, but their membership had consisted of individual members of different churches. The Federal Council, on the other hand, included official representatives of the churches themselves.

While the Federal Council was not exclusively an instrument of the social gospel, it was brought into being largely by the forces of social Christianity. Its first major efforts were in the area of social and economic concerns. At its first meeting in 1908, the Council adopted a report on "The Church and Modern Industry" which represented social gospel attitudes. It also adopted a "Social Creed of the Churches" which, after some revision in 1912, remained the official policy statement of the Federal Council for a generation.[15]

The Federal Council met its first practical test when its Com-

mission on the Church and Social Service investigated a major
strike at Bethlehem Steel in 1910. The fact-finding committee
issued a lengthy report with recommendations to the churches of
Bethlehem, Pennsylvania, to the Council, and to the general public. It investigated charges that the local ministers were unsympa-
thetic to labor and found that some of the accusations were un-
warranted. In its recommendations, the committee called for
abolition of the twelve-hour day and the seven-day week. The
objective and factual character of the report won it a wide and
respectful hearing although it provoked some angry and hostile
response from management and other conservative quarters.[16]
Before World War I, then, the Christian concern for social justice
was imbedded not only in the structure of every major denomination but in the first official interdenominational agency of American Protestantism.

THEOLOGICAL FOUNDATIONS

It was also during this period that the social outlook of the movement received some theological grounding. The earlier writers on
Christian social issues had either been preoccupied with specific
problems, as Washington Gladden had been, or, like Richard Ely,
they were fumbling for new social science tools. Most of their
theological views were inherited and were seldom subjected to
rigorous analysis. As a group, they tended to be more open to
the findings of German biblical scholarship than earlier generations. Yet there was little in their theology that was new. The
considerable criticism of the social gospel that developed in later
years often failed to take this fact into consideration. The failings
of social gospel theology were, on the whole, inherited failings.
Their own inadequacies were shared, for the most part, by their
conservative opponents.

The theological heritage of the social gospel was late nineteenth-century Protestant liberalism. The theological views of the

socially conservative Henry Ward Beecher were indistinguishable from those of Washington Gladden. Both men were equally under the influence of evolutionary thought which, when combined with native American optimism, produced the characteristic American belief in progress. Both believed in an immanent God, working in the processes of nature and history. Both were convinced of man's potentiality for creative response to the challenges of life. Both saw religion primarily as ethical stance and a Christian as one who follows Christ. Both were impatient with traditional dogmas and both rejected the doctrine of original sin.[17]

To this immanentist view of God, the social gospel added the conviction that humanity is a corporate entity, that society is an organism. This idea was not so much a product of the study of social science, although traces of the idea can be found in Herbert Spencer. It was rather a deduction from the belief that God is active in society, for if God is equally active in all men, then all men are bound together in solidarity. The kingdom of God, thus, is the working out of God's activity in the processes of history.

Professor Charles Hopkins points out that "the presence of the divine in society naturally tended to level the old barriers between sacred and secular. . . . 'There is no sacredness about the church that ought not to be attached to the chamber of commerce,' declared Philip S. Moxom." [18] St. Paul's analogy of the church as the body of Christ was applied to the whole society by Gladden and Rauschenbusch.[19] This concern for the whole of society as God's sphere of activity undergirded the efforts of the social gospel pioneers to reform that society and to make it conform to their vision of the kingdom.

Walter Rauschenbusch, the most important spokesman for the social gospel position, both reinforced and challenged this theological framework. After graduating from the Rochester Theological Seminary, where his father taught in the German-speaking department, Rauschenbusch was called to a small Baptist congregation in Hell's Kitchen in Manhattan. There he worked and struggled among his poverty-stricken parishioners for more than ten years. He then returned to Rochester, where he taught at the seminary for the rest of his life. His thought was hammered out amid the heartaches and disappointments of his ministry in a deteriorated slum area.

It is no wonder, then, that the optimism of his contemporaries is muted in Rauschenbusch's writings. He shared the current theological outlook, but he modified much and he rejected much more. He was skeptical about the doctrine of progress. He insisted on seeing man under the aspect of original sin. And while he was convinced that the kingdom of God was coming into history, he saw it not in terms of steady progress onward and upward but as crisis and upheaval and the clash of opposing forces.[20]

Rauschenbusch published his first major work, *Christianity and the Social Crisis,* in 1907. Thereafter he was the recognized leader of the social gospel movement. Deeply religious and sensitive to the needs of the time, Rauschenbusch inspired devotion in his followers and respect in his antagonists. He is best known for his last work, *A Theology for the Social Gospel,* published in 1917. Although he was looked upon as the spokesman for the social gospel theology, Rauschenbusch had little effect, even on those who praised his work. His misgivings about the doctrine of progress, his pessimism about the immediate future of American society, his espousal of socialist politics were all largely ignored by a movement that continued to be progressive, optimistic and, as time went on, somewhat conventional.

THE LEAN YEARS OF THE SOCIAL PASSION

World War I brought a sudden halt to reform movements both within and without the church. As socialism was driven underground by its refusal to support the war, many dedicated Christian socialists broke with the church. Progressivism and the New Freedom were abandoned in the fever of the war effort.

The social movement in the churches fared no better. After

the war, the Federal Council performed one of its most distinguished acts of public service. It investigated the steel strike of 1919 and produced a significant report. But this time, the Council's report, which condemned the United States Steel Company, did not rally any substantial segment of public opinion in its favor. It was clear that war-weariness had almost completely destroyed the Protestant social consensus that had been in the process of development.

One reason for the decline of enthusiasm for social concerns was the prohibition movement. Temperance had long been an item on the agenda of social reform. Reformers had seen the demon rum as a burden on the back of the worker, a thief of his money and a master that kept him in bondage. The radical character of the early prohibition movement is indicated by the fact that Frances Willard, the temperance leader, had been an honorary member of the Knights of Labor and had frequently spoken at radical gatherings.[21]

But during the years of the Anti-Saloon League, something happened to the temperance movement. It lost its radical character along with its compassion. It gradually fell into the hands of moralistic conservatives who altered the attitude of the movement, if not its goals. Paul Carter, in a sensitive analysis of this change, points out that "The humanitarian concern for the drunkard as victim was replaced by righteous indignation at the drinker as criminal." [22] It was this moralistic attitude that was able to marshal enough political pressure to force through the Prohibition Amendment and the Volstead Act. The Act was easier to pass than to enforce. Efforts to enforce it absorbed most of the energy and attention of the Protestant crusaders from 1919 to 1933.

The preoccupation of Protestants with the liquor issue is illustrated by the endorsement of Herbert Hoover in 1928 by the *Christian Century,* by then the leading voice in the movement for social Christianity. Donald Meyer reports it as follows:

They were not sure of Hoover on the Kellogg Pact; they were not sure of him on Latin America; they were wary of his views on labor; all in all, they took Al Smith to be the better man. But Smith had chosen the leading issue: Prohibition; and on Prohibition, the *Century* would go for Sahara.[23]

During the prosperous twenties, the social gospel movement was divided and ineffective. Dr. Meyer points out that neither business nor labor nor the church was ready for the kind of proclamation and program that the liberal clergy anticipated. The social gospel ministers believed that their liberal outlook characterized the bulk of the churches. They believed that America was basically Protestant and liberal. By proclaiming their own version of liberal religion and social concern, therefore, they assumed that they would be speaking to the best of the church and the best of the nation. They were unwilling to engage in the really radical, sectarian activity that might cut them off from both church and community. The movement was thus gradually anesthetized and domesticated until it had little to contribute and little chance of being heard.[24]

This is not to say that there was no social activity in the churches during the twenties. There was much of it, but it tended to be isolated from the mainstream of Protestant life. Semiofficial and unofficial organizations continued to work for social and economic goals. The Methodist Federation for Social Service under Harry F. Ward and the Episcopal Church League for Industrial Democracy under William Spofford both enjoyed official protection if not support. Denominational boards and departments of social service and social action continued their work of supervising social service institutions and educating the churches to the needs of society. Above all, the Federal Council continued its work of research and education, working for the abolition of child labor and the twelve-hour day in the steel industry. Churchmen spoke out during the Red scare, the Sacco-Vanzetti case, and other controversies.[25]

At the same time, forces in opposition to the social gospel were being mobilized. They included evangelical Christians for whom the Christian life was a personal and devotional matter without social significance. They included spokesmen for the world of the expert, who were quick to point out that the ministers lacked technical competence in those fields where they were wont to make pronouncements. More important, they included business-men of a conservative bent who resented the way in which the social gospel clergy had been working to curb their unrestrained economic power. All of these groups spoke for powerful forces in American society. Against their combined onslaught, the pro-phetic voice of the churches had a difficult time in making itself heard. In addition, the increasing secularism of the day had well-nigh destroyed the personal authority of the minister that had even induced J. P. Morgan, in an earlier day, to follow the lead-ership of his parish priest.[26]

Moreover, the social gospel itself was becoming acclimatized. Not only were the old causes losing their appeal, but events were often ahead of the thinking of the churches. Clerical crusaders frequently raised their lances to fight battles that had been over for decades. The new problems of unequal distribution of wealth, the divorce of ownership from management, the increasing con-centration of business and, above all, the increasingly reckless manipulation of the Stock Exchange escaped notice or were too baffling to get the consideration they demanded. Prosperity dulled the edge of prophetic criticism of a materialistic culture whose tastes and values were determined largely by a crass and insensi-tive bourgeoisie. As Paul Carter expresses it:

Social reform, the men of '29 felt, was a matter of adjustment within a framework of permanent prosperity. . . . The result was that when, in 1929, the Social Gospel was applied to the problem of economic justice, it was applied in a manner which prevented it from getting to the heart of the problem. The mechanics tinkered with the truck engine while the truck itself approached the edge of the cliff.[27]

REAWAKENING OF SOCIAL CONCERN

The stock-market crash and the ensuing depression shattered the complacency of the churches. There is no indication that socially sensitive Christians saw depression coming any more than Wall Street did. Nor is there any indication that the churches realized the nature and extent of the damage any earlier than anyone else. But in those churches which had a strong social gospel tradition, the response was a reawakening of the social passion and a readiness to call for basic reforms in society to combat the evils of poverty and deprivation. The General Conference of the Methodist Church sent a delegation to Washington to ask for a federal relief program for the unemployed. The *Baptist* editorialized: "We can be . . . sure that in any fair conflict between rich and poor, Jesus could be found on the side of the poor." [28]

By 1932, the tradition of social concern and prophetic criticism was once more alive in the churches. There were specific and concrete issues to be dealt with. American society was clearly in trouble. People were bewildered and disillusioned. Furthermore —and this factor is of no small consequence—the business community that had dominated American society in the twenties was now thoroughly discredited and on the defensive. In this new climate, the social gospel spoke in fresh and lively tones. As a result of this return to new social awareness in the churches, sensitive Protestants were prepared for the coming of the New Deal.

In spite of the fact that the leading social gospel periodical endorsed Herbert Hoover in 1932, most of the socially concerned clergy were aboard the New Deal bandwagon by the end of the hundred days. Oddly enough, their chief criticism of Roosevelt was that he was too conservative, too much tied in with the business interests. This was the ground for most Protestant criticism of the National Recovery Act. The left wing of the social movement had supported the Socialist party in preference to Roosevelt. It was a long time before that segment of Protestantism came to accept the Roosevelt brand of reform. Radical social gospel clergy in the thirties were put in the curious position of defending the New Deal from conservative attack although they themselves were skeptical of its achievements. On the whole, however, the New Deal period marks the acceptance of the federal government as an appropriate instrument of social welfare and reform. The social gospel clergy certainly helped to pave the way for this acceptance on the part of American Protestants.

REINHOLD NIEBUHR'S THEOLOGICAL CRITIQUE

It was during this period that the social gospel came under its most prolonged and critical attack on the theological level. The attack was spearheaded by Reinhold Niebuhr in the early thirties, though he was joined by others as the decade wore on. Because Niebuhr wrote voluminously on many issues, his position is hard to describe in a few paragraphs. Also, his position changed with the times and with his own growing sensitivity and maturity. For a time, he was a socialist with decided Marxist leanings. But as his skepticism of ideologies and utopias grew, he found the socialist position as much of a straitjacket as liberal Protestantism had been.

Reinhold Niebuhr graduated from Yale Divinity School with an education that fitted him for a conventionally liberal social gospel ministry. He was sent to Detroit where, for thirteen years, he served in a working-class parish. While his parish was by no means a slum area, Niebuhr was nonetheless confronted with the realities of economic power in an industrial society in such a way that his idealism and optimism were rendered irrelevant. By the time he went to Union Theological Seminary to teach Christian Ethics in 1928, Niebuhr's intellectual commitment to the doctrines of progressivism and optimism had been undercut by the social realities. Throughout the thirties, he engaged in a running battle with liberal theology, pacifism, and the social gospel.

Niebuhr's critique of liberal religion centered on the themes of God, man, and history. Niebuhr restated the biblical doctrine of God's transcendence, rejecting the immanentism of the social gospel. God is not to be equated with the spiritual forces of righteousness and humanitarianism. He stands above and beyond man, judging and redeeming. Niebuhr insisted that biblical faith requires that God be understood as a person who possesses his own freedom and who acts historically to heal the breach between man and himself.[29]

Liberal theology had overemphasized the goodness of man, Niebuhr believed, and did not take seriously the biblical understanding of human sinfulness. Yet the biblical view of man as sinner is corroborated not only by the evidence of history but also by the evidence of self-examination. For Niebuhr, however, the most important fact about man was neither his goodness nor his sinfulness, but his freedom. It is because of his radical freedom that man inclines toward sinfulness, Niebuhr maintained. And it is because of this same freedom that man has the capacity to rise above himself, to transcend his own interests and to act lovingly and unselfishly. Therefore, sin cannot be eradicated unless man's freedom is eradicated at the same time. It was Niebuhr's restatement of the doctrine of man as sinner that attracted wide attention—and much criticism—because it flew directly in the face of most contemporary Christian thought as well as denying the preconceptions of secular humanism. Yet Niebuhr did not deny man's capacity for goodness. In fact, he pointed out that "The Christian view of human nature is involved in the paradox of claiming a higher stature for man and of taking a more serious view of his evil than other anthropology." [30]

A third point in Niebuhr's critique was his rejection of the doctrine of progress in history. This assertion too was controversial, since it called into question one of America's oldest and most cherished convictions. Niebuhr did not see history as moving in a straight upward line of development, nor did he see historical fulfillment just ahead. In biblical terms, he saw only the perennial contest of good and evil, but with no clear distinction as to which was which. Movements for justice bring injustice. Movements for freedom bring bondage. Movements for peace breed wars. Niebuhr's view of history went back to St. Augustine. It was couched in terms of irony and paradox, both frustrating categories for Americans who have always been accustomed to thinking in simple and straightforward terms.

Niebuhr's theological insights had a maturing and sobering effect on all American Protestantism. No religious thinker in the twentieth century has had so wide and varied an impact. Even the conservatives who damned him found him useful. Liberals who rejected his theology were forced to respect his political activities and his social criticism. Secularists who could never quite understand his theological preoccupations found themselves in substantial agreement with his political and historical analysis. Niebuhr himself has pointed out that some of the most sympathetic reaction to his views has come from historians and political scientists, the two disciplines that have been most critical of contemporary culture, perhaps because they are ". . . closer to the historical and political realities which refute modern illusions." [31]

Niebuhr's theological position might seem to produce a quietism that repudiates the social-reforming tradition of American Protestantism. Nothing could be further from the truth. Niebuhr himself has been active in political affairs all of his life. He was one of the founders of Americans for Democratic Action (ADA), the moderately leftish branch of democratic liberalism. This activity is not, for him, merely a holdover from a time when he held other opinions. Rather, it stems directly from his views on God, man, and history.

Since man is a sinner, he can never be completely trusted with power. His social arrangements will never reach the ideal. At the same time, some social evils can be corrected. Some measure of proximate justice is attainable. Therefore, a man must be willing to do what he is able to do within the framework of the political and historical possibilities. He may create new problems while trying to solve old ones, but he must be willing to take that risk. He may utterly fail to overcome existing evils, but he will be judged by God, not by history.

Then too, a man who knows himself to be a sinner will approach his historical responsibilities with a new spirit, the spirit of repentance and humility. The vice of virtuous people is the pride that their virtue engenders. Righteous man easily forgets his own sinfulness. Social reformers are not immune to the virus of self-pride. The crusading spirit, the fanatical spirit, the messianic spirit are all ruled out of the Christian perspective because they all grow out of man's unwillingness to admit his own sinfulness.

The Christian view of man, according to Niebuhr, leads to a chastened sense of limitation that produces patience, forbearance, and a willingness to adjust and compromise. His outlook has often been termed "political realism" without the connotation of power-centered cynicism. Whatever shape the Christian social passion assumes in our generation will be largely the result of his work.

SOCIAL CONCERN IN AN AGE OF AFFLUENCE

The postwar decade of the 1950's resembles the 1920's when one concentrates on the economic scene. Both were times of prosperity in which labor was quiescent and conservative. Both saw strikes and discontent, to be sure, but the mood in both eras was fundamentally one of complacency. The economic pie was getting bigger; it was hardly worth fighting over the size of one's share. Consequently, the Christian movement for social action and reform lost momentum. As American society underwent some of the most far-reaching changes in its history, the inevitable dislocations tended to turn men's thoughts inward. Social change brought on a new search for personal identity, evidenced in the nostalgia of the Billy Graham crusades, the desperate optimism of Norman Vincent Peale's cult of "Positive Thinking," the official "piety along the Potomac," and the collegiate searching for "Who am I?" in psychiatric and existential terms.

There were few causes in the fifties for which a man would lay down his life or even take up a burden. For most middle-class Americans, life was reducible to a routine that brought economic returns but which was relatively unsatisfying to the person. "The mill" and "the rat race" were contemporary terms for what had once been thought of as a "vocation." Increasingly, young college students looked with horror on the world they were about to enter and resisted making their commitment to it—by playing "beatnik" if they were especially rebellious or perhaps merely staying over in graduate school for a time if they were less flamboyant in their rejection of middle-class culture.

Again, as in the twenties, the social message of the churches was muted. Not that it was completely absent. Many a struggling suburban pastor would flay the social sins of his congregation, only to be complimented for his dynamic preaching style. There was much criticism of the religious revival, so much so that a sensitive, book-reading Christian might feel just a little abashed if he continued to go to church. Strangely, most of the criticism of religion came from the clergy. Most of the denunciation of the church was made on theological grounds. Conversely, most of the Protestant social criticism was directed against Protestantism's ecclesiastical institutions. The gist of the criticism was that the church was merely acting as the moral guardian of a sick culture. The criticism had its point and it has yet to be adequately answered.

Perhaps this level of criticism reveals the theological gap which has always been most pronounced in American Protestantism: its deficient doctrine of the church. So long as the institutional apparatus is seen as the primary meaning of church, whether explicitly or unconsciously, then the ecclesiastical institution will continue to be either the object of idolatrous veneration or the object of prophetic scorn and denunciation—or both, paradoxically, at the same time.

During the long history of the social gospel movement, the number of Christians who were effectively touched by its doctrines is difficult to assess. Most writers agree that the movement never constituted a majority in American Protestantism. Yet at many points the social passion controlled the power centers of the churches—and still does. Therefore, the social gospel message was proclaimed with more force and power than the number of its adherents would have led one to expect.

THE PRESENT STATUS OF CHRISTIAN SOCIAL CONCERN

The level of social concern is once more on the rise in American Protestantism. It is feeding on the general sense of malaise in American life, the sense that there is still much unfinished business. The postwar complacency is on the wane and Americans are again beginning to face a host of large and complex social issues. Protestant voices are once more calling attention to the ills of society and are pointing to danger signs for the future. The fact that the National Council of Churches of Christ, successor to the old Federal Council, is still being labeled as "socialistic" and even "communistic" by the guardians of American conservatism indicates that the voice of the church's social conscience is not completely silent.

But there is one great difference in today's Christian social concern. It is much more sensitive to the ambiguities inherent in all social, economic, and political issues. The moral issues are by no means clear. There are few obvious heroes or villains. The old distinctions are quite irrelevant to the present. It is hard to distinguish a "left" or a "right," a set of "oppressors" or a set of "oppressed."

This may be why the churches have thrown themselves so passionately into the movement for Negro rights. Here is a movement in which one can tell the "goodies" from the "baddies." It is easy to distinguish heroic Negroes and civil rights workers from the villainous segregationists and the cowardly moderates. The traditional moralistic American liberal could understand such a cause and could throw himself unreservedly into it. In a similar vein, Protestants have begun to tackle the problems of urbanization but, as we shall see, they have already got beyond the point where the issues can be interpreted as a simple battle between predatory landlords and the exploited poor.

The most significant problems facing America resist any formulation in simple-minded, moralistic terms. Urbanization, technological change, population mobility, automation, unemployment, poverty, affluence, institutionalization, mass communications, social disorganization, leisure, boredom, delinquency, crime—all these issues call for understanding based on vast amounts of information. The kind of technical competence that they require is likely to elude the prophet and moral teacher.

For this reason, socially concerned Christians today are more ready to ally themselves with the social scientists, whose task it is to uncover the information and to discover the principles by which men can come to understand the issues that confront them. Churchmen are more willing today than ever to accept the expertise of the scientific investigator and to base their social judgment on the facts provided by the psychologist, the sociologist, the economist, and the political scientist. While it is clear that there are still moral issues which have to be faced out of a sense of Christian responsibility for society, yet it is also clear that the moral issues are imbedded in complex technical problems that can be unraveled only by the scientist who is trained for the task.

At the same time, it should be pointed out that this reliance on the insights of social science is currently being challenged by a whole new approach to social reform. Just within the past several years, a chasm has begun to open up in the ranks of American reformers. On the one side stand the traditional proponents of rational, orderly progress. They tend to accept the need for government participation in the reform process, but usually see that participation in administrative terms. They rely on professional expertise, particularly that of the social scientist, to delineate problems and to propose solutions. Their solutions can be enshrined in legislative programs which, when properly administered, produce the desired result. This was the way of the New Deal and of the civil rights movement, at least in its early days. Until very recently, most liberals would have accepted this description as the way to "do reform."

But today there is a considerable—and growing—body of opinion which rejects this procedure as arrogant and paternalistic on the ground that it fails to take into account the felt needs and desires of the people who will be most affected by the proposed programs. A more authentic mode of operation, in this view, would be to create channels by which those people who are the objects of reform programs could participate in the process of developing the programs. Thus there has been widespread controversy in President Johnson's Poverty Program over the question of whether the poor should be represented on the boards, committees, and other local organizations which determine policies and decide priorities.

There are genuine values in this new "participatory democracy," to be sure. It affirms and safeguards the dignity and worth of even the poorest and lowliest member of society. It poses a fundamental challenge to the built-in assumption of most middle-class reformers that "everyone really wants to be like us." Then, too, it attempts to uphold in practice the ideology of democracy in an area of life where the democratic conviction really matters.

At the same time, the practice of such a ruthless brand of democracy raises some serious questions for the future. If middle-class politics has perhaps overstressed the building of consensus, the new democratic politics puts too much premium on the inherent value of conflict. If the traditional emphasis on rational and scientific solutions to social problems raises the specter of dehumanizing bureaucratic control, this new way of doing things may too readily accept irrationality as a guiding social principle. Its result may well prove to be a new wave of demagoguery which, in its own way, can be just as destructive of persons as was old-fashioned bureaucratic arrogance.

It would seem that the nation is in for a protracted period of turbulent struggle in the social realm as this controversy works itself out. We may well wish that it were not so. Participatory democracy may seem to be a regression from the relative maturity of our consensus-politics of recent years. The fact remains, however, that many people, particularly the urban poor, have now found their voice and will no longer be satisfied to have benevolent professional administrators solve their problems for them.

In a curious way, the self-conscious independence of the poor, which is being advocated by the "new left," is based on concepts that closely resemble those of the "old right." The language may differ, but the content is the same. Both views express the same suspicion of the middle-class reformer. Even more fundamental to both views is a hostility to the idea that social problems are amenable to scientific solutions developed by people outside the situation. It will be interesting to see how long it takes for these two antagonistic traditions to begin to recognize their thinly disguised affinities.

It is far too soon to say what the church can contribute to this dialogue within the ranks of reform. It is easy to say that the church must seek some middle ground which will reconcile the opposites and affirm the values of each position. This may, indeed, be the case. But to reach such a quick and painless conclusion would be to beg the real questions rather than dealing responsibly with them.

What is presently needed, of course, is for the church to turn its attention once again to the long-neglected issue of social thought. This new dialogue raises fundamental questions about the nature of man, of society and of the responsible use of power. It has been many years since the church has been required to devote serious attention to these basic theoretical concerns. The time has come, however, when this whole area of thought must be opened for re-examination in order that the church may be alive to the issues of the day and may speak to those issues in coherent terms.

CONTEMPORARY PROTESTANT SOCIAL CONCERN

Although the dimensions of the social issue have changed, and the theological grounding of the social passion has been transformed, I am convinced that the social-gospel movement has had a profound and lasting effect upon American Protestantism. Today, most American Christians who take their religions seriously do, in fact, see some relationship between their religious convictions and their social values and attitudes. To this extent, it may be said that the social gospel has done its work well. Human nature being what it is, of course, many of those same people will interpret the social consequences of the gospel in the light of their own interests and social conditioning. Even a socially aware religion can be used to support a political, economic, or class interest.

Perhaps the most significant social task of the church is to point continually to this conjunction of conviction and self-interest in order to free the gospel from all false social, economic, and political solutions. This does not mean that Christians must reject the world. On the contrary, it means that relevance is to be sharply distinguished from accommodation, and that all social, economic, and political interests are to be judged in the name of the Lord.

7 THE URBAN MISSION COMES OF AGE

OUR GENERATION is witnessing a remarkable display of interest in the ministry of the church to the city. Throughout America, city churches are learning to understand their Christian mission in terms of the needs of their community. Churches in the deteriorated "inner city" are learning to conduct ministries to the poor and the hopeless of all races. Wealthy suburban churches contribute money and the efforts of their laymen to help provide resources and leadership for churches which face overwhelming problems in their inner-city ministry. Denominational boards and committees, often with large budgets and competent professional direction, study the needs of their urban areas in order to plan a coherent strategy for the city work of the churches.

This movement has attracted enough attention, both within the church and in the secular press, to make it look like a revolution. American Protestantism, after all, has always been rural in character and preference. Protestantism unavoidably looks back to a simpler time, the time of its early American successes.

At that time, the United States was a nation of small towns and countryside. Cities of over 10,000 population were almost unheard of in the early part of the nineteenth century. While the contrasting stories of New England and the southern colonies indicate that religion prospered in settled rather than sparsely populated areas, those early settlements were quite small. They did not present any of the problems that have since come to be associated with urbanization. Furthermore, the first real crisis faced by American Protestantism, the crisis of the frontier, served to turn men's eyes away from the city and its problems.

PROTESTANT UNEASINESS IN THE URBAN ENVIRONMENT

As a result of its great missionary activity on the frontier, Protestantism in America developed most significantly in the rural areas. Because it helped to shape the moral climate of the American small town, it found that climate congenial. By contrast, the growing cities of the later nineteenth century seemed to Protestant churchmen to be full of agonizing problems and forces that boded ill for the future of the church. The prevailing view that God made the country while man made the city was not complimentary to the city, nor was it intended to be. For the fact is that American Protestantism early developed a suspicion, even a hostility, toward the city, seeing in it only misery and poverty, on the one hand, and worldliness and materialism, on the other.

This antiurban bias was not confined to the churches. Indeed, Morton and Lucia White have recently pointed out that American intellectuals have generally harbored a deep-seated antagonism toward the city.[1] At the very time when cities were coming to dominate the American scene, namely the latter half of the nineteenth century, one would have had to look hard to discover a first-rate novel, poem, or painting depicting the city as anything other than a sinkhole of iniquity. There was no celebration of the glories of the city, no praise of its cultural advantages, no recognition that civilization had anything at all to do with the *civitas*.

We have already discussed the rise of industrialization during this period. With the growth of manufacturing, cities increased in population with incredible rapidity. The increase consisted of two disparate elements. Farmers and small-town dwellers were forced into the cities to look for work. They brought with them the traditional Protestant suspicion of the city and a nostalgia for the ways of the small town. Then too, immigrants crowded into the cities, often in response to aggressive recruiting campaigns initiated by the manufacturing interests. These new citizens came mostly from southern and eastern Europe; they were predominantly Roman Catholic and few of them spoke English. Thus there grew up in the cities a polyglot population that baffled the native Protestants, who retained their preference for the small, homogeneous community as the model of the Christian society.

This is not to say that Protestantism had no strength in the cities. On the contrary, many city churches were large, strong, and affluent. But changes were occurring. The older churches which had long been dominant in the eastern cities, the Congregational, Unitarian, Episcopal, and Presbyterian churches, lost ground as newer churches grew and spread. By the time of the Civil War, the Baptists and Methodists had become the largest Protestant denominations. While the great increase in their membership occurred first on the frontier, as the century wore on they began to grow in the cities as well. Originally, both the Baptist and the Methodist churches were composed primarily of members of the lower class: small farmers, tradesmen, and workers. But as time went on, perhaps as a result of the discipline that stemmed from their religion, many of the descendants of the early Baptists and Methodists became established in the city as skilled workers and small businessmen and many of them rose rapidly to affluence and power. The problem inherent in this process had been anticipated by John Wesley himself when he wrote: "The Methodists in every place grow diligent and frugal; consequently they increase in goods. Hence they proportionally increase in pride, in anger, in the desire of the flesh, the desire of the eyes and the pride of life. So, although the form of religion remains, the spirit is swiftly vanishing away." [2]

In the post-Civil War period, Protestants made up the bulk of the upper and middle classes. Their attitudes set the moral tone for urban society and their values tended to become the values of the culture. Yet at the same time, they were deeply immersed in the new industrialism, mostly as proprietors, financiers, small capitalists or, at least, hopeful entrepreneurs. In their church life, they tended to maintain the habits and the ideology of the small town. They held revival meetings. They put on church suppers. They tried to keep a style of life that would protect their members from the cultural changes inevitable in city living. While they acted as a useful bridge between older rural values and urban living, at the same time they set up barriers that prevented the accommodation of small-town mentalities to the realities of urbanization.

Hence the churches had no response to make as their more affluent members joined the rush for the almighty dollar that was characteristic of the gilded age. Andrew Carnegie proclaimed his gospel of wealth in 1889 and there was no theological voice raised in the church to contest his view that free enterprise was the lifeblood of society. When the more rabid followers of Charles Darwin and Herbert Spencer claimed that poverty, while perhaps lamentable, was a necessary and valuable consequence of the struggle for existence, the churches for the most part were silent.

But this picture of a complacent and irrelevant church can easily be overdrawn, for here and there voices were raised in protest against the evils prevalent in American society. Protestantism never abandoned the working class completely. There were some churches that continued to minister to working-class neighborhoods. There were some clergy who did not subscribe to the convenient morality of the business class. And there was a significant minority movement that was concerned to help the church face the issues posed by the new shape of American society.

The various aspects of this movement included a ministry to the urbanized rural Protestant who had been cut off from his religious heritage; a ministry to the newer immigrants from Europe; a concern for the most poor and helpless elements of the city population; and care for the most obvious casualties of urban life. While this movement lacked definite shape and coherence, these various aspects may best be seen as parts of a total response of the whole church to a new social situation. The parts of the movement interacted at times while at other times they pursued their independent existence. The social gospel, which addressed itself primarily to the industrial situation, has already been discussed. In this chapter we will be concerned primarily with the churches' search for new forms of urban ministry.

EARLY EFFORTS AT URBAN MINISTRY

As early as 1836, a ministry to the working class had been attempted by Orestes Brownson, transcendentalist, Jacksonian reformer, journalist, and future convert to Roman Catholicism. Brownson founded in Boston a Society for Christian Union and Progress, an unusual sort of church in which he proposed to minister to both spiritual and material needs, to wed Christian faith to social reform.[3] Brownson's society did not outlive his own brief participation in it, but it represents a very early attempt to grapple with an issue that was to occupy the Protestant reformers for the rest of the century.

Another pioneer in the city church movement was William Augustus Muhlenburg, best known in Episcopal circles for his advocacy of church union and co-operative effort under the banner of "Evangelical Catholicism." In 1845, he founded a new parish in New York City, the Church of the Holy Communion, in which he developed a constellation of institutions and activities that were to provide a model for later and better organized

attempts to deal with urban problems. Like Brownson, Muhlenburg allowed no rented pews in his church so that the poor would
always feel welcome. He founded St. Luke's Hospital and developed an order of deaconesses to operate it. He founded a
model community outside the city as a refuge for slum dwellers.
The community included cottages, a church, a home for crippled
children, and a home for the aged.[4]

The leading nondenominational organization concerned with
urban evangelism was likewise founded well before the Civil War.
This was the Young Men's Christian Association, which was intended to reach young men who had moved to the city and had
thereby removed themselves from the moral influence of their
home church. The YMCA was founded in London in 1844 and
came to America in 1851, when a chapter was opened in Boston.
Thereafter, it spread rapidly to other cities and soon developed a
strong national organization. At first, it engaged in general missionary endeavors, including work among the poor, but in the
years following the Civil War, the Association gradually limited
itself to work among young, middle-class males. In this way, it
avoided conflict with the missionary societies of the several
churches. Once it had restricted the scope of its work, the YMCA
began to receive the hearty support of the churches.

From the late 1860's, the YMCA program centered around
a central building with facilities for housing, recreation, worship,
and education. The Association engaged in massive fund-raising
activities for which it was able to attract significant leadership
and support from the business community. There is little doubt
that the YMCA was able to reach people who were not being
touched by the churches. At the same time, the tenuousness of
the Association's church relationship posed the inevitable problem of the nature and shape of its Christian commitment. As the
years went on, the YMCA's program developed more and more
in the direction of broad social welfare, education, and recreation. The evangelical impetus which had founded it became sub-
merged to the point where, in the 1960's, the word "Christian"
was finally stricken from its pledge of membership.

PROTESTANT URBAN ENGAGEMENT

As we have seen, the social gospel developed a critique of the industrialism which was breeding a staggering collection of problems in the American city. At the same time, others in the churches were coming to grips with the most serious of these problems without necessarily engaging in any movement for the general reform of society. Their activities were developed in response to obvious and specific needs. They began in the local churches, primarily as a response to that perennial problem of the American city: the changing neighborhood.

A local Protestant church tends to minister to a gathered group of people rather than to a territory. Nonetheless, in the mid-nineteenth century, the limitations of transportation required that most church members live in the immediate vicinity of the church building. As members grew prosperous and moved into better neighborhoods, they tended to take their church along with them. Thus the usual pattern of church life anticipated that a successful church would move nearly every generation, and many of them did.

But some churches were unable or unwilling to follow after their clientele. They were left with the problem of survival. The best way to survive was to learn how to minister to the new and different people who were then moving into the neighborhood. Since these people tended to be poor, less closely related to the church, uneducated, frequently of foreign birth, in desperate need, and often outspokenly anticlerical, the churches had to find new ways of ministry and new institutional forms to facilitate their new tasks.

THE INSTITUTIONAL CHURCH

The most significant and enduring of these new forms of ministry was the "institutional church" which developed during the last quarter of the century. The institutional church was based on the conviction that, if the church was to win over the poor and laboring classes, it would have to meet them on the level of simple human need. A climate of trust and confidence would have to be established through long and conscientious service to the community. Only then would the traditional hostility of the poor toward the church be overcome.

St. George's Episcopal Church in New York City was the most famous of the early institutional churches. Refusing to move the church out of its changing neighborhood on the East Side of Manhattan, the Vestry in 1880 called as rector the Rev. W. S. Rainsford, an able and energetic young man with considerable experience in church social work and city missions. Rainsford's ideas and forcefulness enabled him to win the respect of many of his most conservative members. He built a large and well-equipped parish hall to house the church's numerous activities. His major emphasis was on education, particularly industrial and business training which, he felt, would prepare working-class people for jobs and advancement. The church also maintained athletic facilities, baths, and meeting areas for numerous special-interest clubs.[5]

Rainsford relied heavily on lay and professional leadership. The parish maintained a deaconess home to house the women who worked there. The clergy likewise lived together, sharing a common life and discipline. More than twenty-five young men were trained for similar work during Rainsford's pastorate.

By the end of the century, St. George's had grown to over 4,000 members and possessed an endowment fund of over

$200,000, a magnificent sum for the period. J. P. Morgan, a member of the Vestry, remained enthusiastic over the achievements of the parish, though some conservative members withdrew their support. Since the parish included such men as Charles A. Dana of the New York *Sun* and Admiral A. T. Mahan, the leading exponent of imperialism by sea power, it is no wonder that the humanitarian concerns of the rector aroused some opposition.

Rainsford had not only a program but a policy and a sense of priorities. He was convinced that the church ought to engage in social welfare projects according to the needs of time and place. Its engagement should be supplemented by its prophetic voice, but it had to do more than merely criticize the existing order. The church needed to provide concrete examples of reform and humanitarianism in action. As other agencies in the community perceive the need and are won over to the program, he pointed out, then the church can gradually turn its projects over to those agencies and seek other tasks itself. Thus the church would not only point the way to reform, but it would always be out in front, blazing the trail.[6]

As other churches began to develop similar programs, the institutional church movement grew in extent and influence. The institutional churches provided a bewildering array of activities appealing to all classes and age groups. There were sewing and cooking classes; classes in the English language, in democracy, in Americanism. There were medical clinics, employment bureaus, lending facilities, bath houses, gymnasiums, girls' boardinghouses. In Philadelphia at the Baptist Temple, the Rev. Russell Conwell started a class in religious instruction that grew into a college which today is Temple University. All major denominations participated in the institutional church movement. This one organizational innovation probably did more than anything else to spread the leaven of humanitarian and social concern throughout Protestantism.

By 1894, the movement was sufficiently widespread to warrant the founding of the Institutional Church League to focus the many experimental programs being generated by churches throughout the land. It was hoped that the result of the League would be a total advance in the field of practical church work.

The League rejected the division of the world into the realms of "sacred" and "secular" and stated in its platform that the institutional church stands for

. . . open church doors every day and all the day, free seats, a plurality of Christian workers, the personal activity of all church members, a ministry to all the community through educational, reformatory and philanthropic channels, to the end that men may be won to Christ and His service, that the Church may be brought back to the simplicity and comprehensiveness of its primitive life, until it can be said of every community, "The Kingdom of Heaven is within you" and Christ is all and in all.[7]

The League issued a monthly paper, the *Open Church,* as an avenue of communication to inform member churches about new programs in other churches. It also did much to encourage the spread of the institutional church idea. By the end of the century, there were 173 institutional churches in existence, though the category is too vague to make adequate reporting possible.[8] Episcopal and Congregational churches led in number. Parish houses were springing up all over the country, a fact which many contemporary churchmen look back upon with some misgiving. Nevertheless, it is clear that by the beginning of the twentieth century, American Protestantism was becoming convinced of the need for the local church to engage in a wider ministry to its community.

EXTRAPAROCHIAL STRATEGIES

The efforts of the local churches, as typified by the institutional church movement, were perhaps the most valuable and enduring response of Protestantism to the urban challenge. But the

Protestant response was by no means limited to the local church. Indeed, many denominations responded more quickly on other institutional levels. On the eve of the Civil War, city mission societies were already engaged in rescue work in some of the larger cities. Denominational efforts were paralleled by similar efforts on a nondenominational basis. The best known of the latter was the New York City Mission and Tract Society.

The city missions engaged in a variety of activities. They provided shelter and food for the down-and-out. Some maintained employment agencies. Others provided classes, lectures, reading rooms, and entertainment. Special needs often resulted in the founding of supplementary institutions. Special ministries were provided, for example, for seamen, prisoners, and other groups not ordinarily reached by the churches. Homes were started for the aged, for the indigent, for unwed mothers, for working girls, and for orphans. Hospitals were founded in the lower-income areas of the large cities long before there was any general public concern for such projects.

The churches responded to the influx of European immigrants by developing missions carried on by ministers trained in the language of the people. At the same time, attempts were made to perpetuate the work by raising up clergy from the immigrant groups themselves. This work was complicated by a number of factors. The language barrier was not inconsiderable. Then too, many of the newer immigrants were Roman Catholics, whether or not they retained any actual relationship to their traditional church. Finally, there were class and cultural differences that set these new groups apart from those who were trying to minister to them. In view of these obstacles, it is remarkable that the foreign-language missions were able to accomplish anything at all.

The immigrant ministry took many forms. Often it meant merely that a local church would make special efforts to welcome immigrant children into the regular activities of the church. Sometimes, the churches provided classes in which immigrants could learn to speak and write English. Some parishes provided worship services in foreign languages. A. I. Abell reports, for example, that St. Bartholomew's Episcopal Church in New York City was equipped to minister in Armenian, Syriac, and Turkish. In some places, special congregations were founded to minister to immigrant groups in their own language. By the end of the century, the Congregationalists maintained 150 German congregations and about a dozen Bohemian churches.[9] The provision of a foreign-language ministry was facilitated by the development of foreign-language departments in many of the seminaries.

The results of this mission to the immigrants are hard to assess. It was no doubt most successful among Germans who were Lutherans already. It succeeded in keeping alive some genuine concern for immigrants among Protestants. It succeeded in converting some immigrants to Protestant Christianity, although the number is probably not large. Perhaps its most significant achievement was the Christian service which it carried on without regard to the immigrant's present or potential membership status. This service reached out to both Catholics and Jews and may at least have served to lead some members of these groups to regard American Protestants as friends and allies.

The Salvation Army was, like the YMCA, an import from England that took root and flourished in the American city of the late nineteenth century. Because it was concerned with those who had fallen furthest and because it used flamboyant techniques to reach them, the Army provoked much criticism and opposition when it first appeared in the United States. Many churchmen resented the undignified street-corner preaching, the willingness of the Army to use saloons as missionary centers, and the sensationalism of the Army's appeal. Professor Abell reports from an early field report made by telegraph: "Sunday glorious smash; 13 in fountain; died hard hallelujah!"[10]

By 1890, however, patient public relations work on the part of the Army's new leader, General Ballington Booth, had smoothed over most of the clerical opposition. The churches began to realize that the Salvation Army was able to reach multitudes who were beyond the reach of the churches themselves. Consequently, they were inclined to accept, and even to imitate, the Army's sensational methods.

The Salvation Army's aims were admittedly limited. It confined itself to the very lowest rung on the social ladder, an area where the competition was not great. It accepted the existing social and economic system, seeking only to rescue the most seriously handicapped victims of the system. Its aims and outlook were therefore conservative, but within the context of those aims and purposes the Army performed a valuable and useful function as, indeed, it still does.

The settlement house, another British importation, developed around the turn of the century. Toynbee Hall in London provided the model for this new instrument of social welfare. Like the institutional church, the settlement house sought to identify itself with its neighborhood, providing a complete schedule of social services and educational programs. The best-known settlement house was Jane Addams' Hull House in Chicago, though many others were developed in the major industrial cities.

Settlement houses were less generally related to churches, though a few were operated by religious organizations. Some were staffed by college students who were thus given their first look at the poverty that was becoming a serious American social problem. The social conscience instilled by these experiences remained with many a successful middle-class business or professional man, providing a leaven of humanitarian concern that often made a reformer out of the type of person who might otherwise have remained most insensitive and complacent.

The first great period of the churches' urban ministry came to a close shortly after the beginning of the new century. World War I brought a virtual end to the urban enthusiasm just as it choked off the social gospel and political progressivism. This is not to say, however, that the churches lost interest in the city. On the contrary, the various institutions that had been created during the previous period—the city mission, the YMCA, the Salvation Army, the institutional church, the settlement house—continued to exist. But there were few new developments, few new institutions created, and few new departures attempted. After the war, the prosperity of the twenties and the issue of prohibition served to turn men's attention elsewhere.

During the depression years, the old institutions continued to function, but only half-heartedly and with seriously reduced budgets. There was little money around for such work and there was an increasing disposition to turn over all social work to the government: federal, state, or local. The church's social service agencies continued to be staffed largely by men who had caught the original enthusiasm in their youth. While many of them retained the enthusiasm, they were all getting older and few young men were coming along to replace them. It began to look as though most of Protestantism had forgotten that cities are full of heartbreak and human misery.

THE ERA OF SUBURBIA

The end of World War II brought to the churches a revival of the domestic concerns that war had brushed into the background. But whereas the preoccupation of the progressive era and the New Deal period had been with the regulation of business and the adjustment of the economy, by the late 1940's American society was showing a flexibility and resilience that would very likely make major social reforms unnecessary in the future. The economy was beginning to produce abundance as the nation entered what Walt W. Rostow calls "the age of high mass-consumption." [11] The only economic problems remaining, it seemed, were to ensure continued full employment and to further equalize the distribution of wealth.

These concerns produced little anxiety in the socially sensitive church leadership. The labor movement was strong and aggressive. The unions could be counted on to speak out for the working man. Then too, the New Deal experience had inspired confidence in the federal government as an agency of reform. It had vast resources at its disposal and would presumably continue to be responsive to human needs. At first glance, there seemed to be little need for the churches to engage in any form of social action.

But new social problems were being created even as old ones were dismissed. The postwar housing shortage touched off a major building boom that changed the face of the nation once more. The massive population shift that occurred after the war has resulted in a large-scale increase in urbanization so that today, more than 75 per cent of the American people live in areas that are officially designated as "metropolitan." [12]

This increasing urbanization was, at first, partially screened by the fact that from 1940 on, most large American cities have been losing population. The new growth was taking place, not in the core cities themselves, but in the surrounding suburban areas. Whole new towns grew up overnight and old towns were transformed as real estate developers built new houses by the hundreds and the thousands. Young couples with small children gratefully moved out of their crowded city apartments to make their homes in the grass-lined streets of suburbia.

The sheen has worn off suburbia by now, so it is hard to recapture the thrill and the promise of suburban life that animated so much of the movement out of the cities. Leading churchmen had long previously pointed to the suburb as the hope and salvation of the city. With the widespread use of the automobile, a working man could hope to live in a small community in a house of his own with his own patch of grass. His children could play outdoors in the fresh air and sunshine. At the same time, he could easily commute to his job in the city, thereby enjoying the advantages of both country and city life. The result would be a return to a society of homeowners, each with a stake in the stability of his community. The church would enjoy the advantage of working in a community where people stayed put and where the overwhelming problems of tenement-house living had been permanently overcome.

It was to be expected, therefore, that as the people moved into the suburbs the churches would move along with them. This is just about what happened. The churches sold their city properties to Negro churches or Pentecostal sects. New church buildings sprang up in the suburbs and the new residents rushed to fill them. The decade of the 1950's was to witness a significant increase in church membership which soon took on the shape of a popular religious revival, the effects of which are still with us.

REVIVAL OF THE URBAN MINISTRY

The suburban population boom took up most of the interest and concern of the Protestant churches. They had to expend great effort to supply the new parishes with clergy, to provide financial support for their building ventures, and to maintain some kind of order in their development. This process so engaged the attention of the churches that their ministry to the city was easily forgotten. In November, 1958, attention was called to this urban neglect by Dr. Truman B. Douglass, Executive Vice-President of the Board of Home Missions of the Congregational Christian Churches. In an article written for *Harper's Magazine,* Dr. Douglass pointed out: "In almost direct proportion to the increasing importance of the city in American culture has been the withdrawal—both physical and spiritual—of the Protestant Church." [13]

Dr. Douglass went on to say that Protestant churches had been moving out of the growing American cities at an alarming rate. He attributed this movement to "an anti-urban bias which has become almost a point of dogma in American Protestantism." [14] Dr. Douglass' outburst attracted considerable attention at the time, largely because his charges were hard to deny. In the light of what we have just said about Protestantism in the nineteenth-century city, it could hardly be maintained that Protestantism had abandoned the city. Yet it was demonstrably true that, as Dr. Douglass wrote, the churches were engaged in a massive withdrawal from the core cities of America. His own figures make his point.

In Detroit, fifty-three churches deserted the heart of the city within a fifteen-year period. The statistics of one denomination's history in New York City show that during the past century in Manhattan and the Bronx it has dissolved fifty-four churches and merged forty-two with other congregations.[15]

By the time that Dr. Douglass' article appeared, however, a new movement was already under way to revive the urban ministry of the Protestant churches. Indeed, Dr. Douglass' article was itself a part of that movement. It is hard to date the beginning of the urban revival because it began quietly, with small, separate projects developing here and there. The movement had picked up considerable momentum before many people were aware that it was in existence. Perhaps the first step was a reawakening of interest in the inner city. As in the nineteenth century, there was a concern to restore life to a number of dying city churches and to prepare churches in rapidly changing neighborhoods to adjust to their new situations. At the same time, there was an interest in developing radically new and different forms of ministry that would be appropriate to those badly deteriorated areas of the city in which the churches maintained little or no ministry at all.

The East Harlem Protestant Parish was one of these new, experimental ministries. It opened in August, 1948, in a deteriorated section of New York City where, in an area of little more than one square mile, 215,000 people were crowded.[16] It was an area of low incomes, disintegrating buildings, congestion, disease, unemployment, delinquency, and social disorganization. The older Protestant churches had all moved out and only a small percentage of the population had any identification with any church.[17]

The East Harlem Protestant Parish was reminiscent of earlier

Protestant efforts in urban ministry. Like the St. George's of Rainsford's day, it made use of a team ministry the members of which were committed to a common discipline. Part of this discipline was financial. Staff members were paid according to their need. Fees for lectures or writing were put into the general fund. The discipline also included a weekly sharing of the Holy Communion and the observance of other personal and corporate devotional practices.

The Parish was also committed to a program of social action which involved the staff in politics. This political participation has provoked criticism of the Parish in some church circles, but it has proved an effective means for identifying the Parish with its community.

But the Parish is more than a revival of old and accepted techniques. Its very inception was unusual in that it was the result of a planned strategy to put the Protestant Church to work in a seriously depressed neighborhood. An interdenominational board worked for months in advance to lay plans for the Parish. Its interdenominational character was also unusual. Four churches co-operated in the founding of the Parish and four others joined the project later.

At the beginning, the Parish had no church building at all. Only later was a defunct Presbyterian church building added to the Parish facilities. The lack of a building at the beginning was no accident. The staff preferred to rent store-fronts to avoid identification of the Parish with middle-class, local church Protestantism.

Parish activities have included regular worship and instruction plus a wide variety of less conventional activities. Lay teams have been organized to canvass entire blocks of residents. A special ministry to drug addicts has been initiated. Legal aid and credit union facilities have been set up. Retreats and family camping have been carried on at a center owned by the Parish. A community summer youth program has been established for children.

Along with these activities, there has been an attempt to understand the implications of the work of the Parish. Social scientists have been invited to study the Parish, its community and its operations, and to evaluate its effectiveness. The staff have engaged in theological study and reflection and have made themselves available to church bodies throughout America in order to share their thinking and to receive criticism.[18] This process has helped to avoid the isolation into which such a specialized ministry could easily fall. George W. Webber, one of the early leaders of the Parish, is convinced that the East Harlem Parish has much to teach the American church. He sees the issue of depersonalization as the chief problem of East Harlem and he asserts that it is also the chief problem of America at large. As he has stated the case: "If . . . depersonalization does in fact characterize our whole society, then East Harlem is not a backwater of modern America, a place where certain problems have not been solved, but rather a place in which one sees more obviously than elsewhere the basic problems with which our society is confronted." [19]

Grace Episcopal Church in the Van Vorst section of Jersey City, New Jersey, is a conventional Episcopal parish with a long history in its present location. Yet like the East Harlem Parish, it was deliberately chosen in 1949, after extensive survey work, to be the location for another attempt to minister to a deteriorated neighborhood. Similar too is its commitment to minister to a whole geographical area, rather than just to its own members. Grace Church encountered many of the same community problems as those of East Harlem: crime, delinquency, drunkenness, prostitution, brutality. Many of the same techniques were employed: neighborhood visitations, social service work, activities for children and teen-agers, summer neighborhood programs, and the traditional church functions of corporate worship and religious instruction.

Like the East Harlem Parish, Grace Church had a team ministry consisting of priests, nuns, and the wives of the clergy. Local laymen were trained for parish duties in preference to hiring additional staff. One further innovation was that the clergy wives maintained an "open rectory," inviting people to come in casually at almost any time for refreshments and conversation.[20]

These two well-known church projects share many of the characteristics of the new urban movement. Both are directed to the entire community in which they are located. Both maintain team ministries. Both make use of the insights of modern social science. Both are heavily supported by funds from denominational and other outside sources. Both carry on educational, recreational, and social service programs. Both see the training of clergy and lay leaders as a part of their mission. Both see in their work an opportunity for American Protestantism to learn something about the urban ministry. Both have, in turn, been seen as models of effective urban work by other churches which have been thus inspired to develop their own plans for inner-city work.

GROWTH OF THE URBAN MOVEMENT

During the years in which the work of parishes like Grace Church and East Harlem was taking shape, the impulse toward urban ministry was growing and expanding. Churches in cities throughout the country began to reconsider plans for moving out of the city in favor of finding ways to minister to their present neighborhoods. A great variety of experiments were tried out. The realization grew that urban society is not merely a description of the inner city, but that it encompasses large and important segments of American life. Denominations consequently began to see the need to develop a missionary strategy for entire metropolitan areas and to provide aid and comfort to local churches as they embarked on their urban ministry. In 1950, a Division of Urban Industrial Church Work was established in the National Council of the Protestant Episcopal Church. Later that same year, the National Council of Churches set up a Department of Urban Church.[21] The home missions departments of other denominations added staff members specifically to work with problems of urban society.

Out of these new agencies has grown a considerable literature designed to acquaint city church leaders with the nature of their problems and with techniques which might be helpful in dealing with them. The congregation is urged to base its ministry on the needs of its community. The local church is seen as a bridge to community social agencies. Churches are instructed in the use of the self-study, which involves the gathering of data on population, age, sex and racial composition, occupational information, and community resources. The self-study can give a local church a more accurate picture of its neighborhood and a more realistic view of its own place in the community. Used properly, the self-study can provide a sound basis on which a ministry to the community can be developed.

At the same time, there has been an increasing demand for church planning on a broader level than that of the local church. "No one parish," writes Paul Moore, "will have a comprehensive inner-city ministry. For the urban problem must be met by a body of broader organizational scope—that is the diocese, district, or presbytery." [22] But even these traditional units may not be large enough to meet the needs of the present. G. Paul Musselman has called for the creation of new church organizations with a mandate to plan strategically for the newly emerging "strip cities" which result when contiguous metropolitan areas begin to grow into each other.[23]

One reason for the emphasis on citywide church organization is the growing realization that only units of such size and scope can participate responsibly in citywide attacks on the problems of metropolis. As one handbook on church planning suggests:

Planners, renewal leaders, welfare councils and other related agencies are asking that the churches work in closer co-ordination with them. The Church has a responsibility to relate itself to these agencies and to strengthen their work in the community. It is almost impossible for separate denominations, much less separate congregations, to do this in an effective way.[24]

This is not only a plea for bigger organization. It is a call to the churches to participate in the urban-planning process itself.

Many contemporary Protestant observers of the changing city would agree with Joseph Sittler's conclusion:

What we are actually experiencing . . . is not an organic and intelligent evolution of the city. We are seeing its destruction. . . . The homogenization of the city, and the standardization of its sections according to the sole norm of profitable land use and commercial convenience, is accomplishing a destruction of the city vast in scope, fierce in pace and ruthless in its human hurt.[25]

The church's responsibility, according to Sittler, must go beyond caring for the social casualties of city life. It must include ". . . bringing under radical question the very structures of politics and economics which guarantee by their monomaniac reading of human life that this destructive procedure will go on and on." [26]

The church's interest in city planning stems from its interest in finding the best possible locations for new church buildings. The concern has since gone far beyond such simple institutional self-seeking. Already the churches have developed a lively interest in the radical process of redesigning the urban environment to make possible a more fitting habitation for human beings.

At the same time, the planning process itself is particularly open to the possibility of concerned participation by the churches. In recent years, city planners have begun to move away from reliance on preconceived, prepackaged master plans which had to be sold to a skeptical public. According to the current view, interested individuals and groups should be encouraged to contribute their ideas and criticisms while the plan is still in a fluid state. As city planner Perry Norton has put it:

Not only is this movement . . . evidence of a new and meaningful acceptance of community planning; it is also becoming the means for opening the new forum of communication. . . . Now as never before it is possible for groups and social organizations, each with its own special responsibilities, to come together for a fruitful sharing of basic goals and objectives.[27]

From this perspective, it can be conceded that the churches do have a contribution to make to the planning process. It is no less than a function of the moral and ethical leadership which society has a right to expect of the church. The specific nature of that contribution is less clear. No doubt the churches can, by acting together, provide a measure of disinterested criticism and support. They might also help to create a public climate favorable to the renewal of the city. Gibson Winter, sociologist and priest, has suggested that if the churches wish to provide guidance in the metropolitan community, they must:

(1) affirm community by forming a ministry to the whole metropolis; (2) offer a vision and experience of metropolitan community by exemplifying a community; (3) inform the metropolitan struggle for community with [their] own prophetic concern for the common good of the metropolitan area.[28]

Although it is too soon to tell how effective will be the movement to involve the churches in urban planning, hopeful signs have already appeared. Some churches have begun to add professional planners to their urban work staffs. At least this move should guarantee that, whatever the nature and scope of the churches' participation in the city-planning process in the future, it will be based on sound professional advice as well as a kind disposition.

THEOLOGY CONFRONTS URBANIZATION

The interest of the churches in urban planning has begun to evolve into a concern for the larger phenomenon of urbanization itself. That concern is producing, in turn, a theological critique of the role of the church in a secularized, urbanized culture. The dim outlines of this critique are just barely discernible, but so far two elements begin to stand out as primary. One is a fundamental theological affirmation of urban culture as a valid context for the

Christian life. The other is a critical questioning of the adequacy of the church's traditional forms of ministry.

The contemporary acceptance of the city is perhaps the most striking aspect of this new urban awareness. The typically Protestant attitude toward the city in the nineteenth century was, as we have seen, fundamentally hostile. The pioneers of the nineteenth-century urban ministry were able to see the growing importance of the city in determining the shape and direction of American life, but they were mostly impressed by the overwhelming problems presented by the city. Recent Protestant writers, on the other hand, have begun to stress the opportunities and the attractions of city life.[29] The city is the realm of education, of the arts, of literature and the theater. It is the bearer of the best in human culture. It is not only Babylon, it is also Jerusalem. The Bible opens in the Garden, but it concludes in the Holy City. City man looks ahead; he is open to the new and different. His virtues are sociability, interrelatedness, tolerance, and freedom. As Langmead Casserley has pointed out, "The real task of spirituality and religion is to consecrate and exalt the values of the city."[30]

Even the frequently noted impersonality of the city is seen as an advantage by Peter Berger, who writes:

The city is the locale of freedom. And it is precisely because of its mass character that this is so. . . . Modern urban society provides quite new and highly significant opportunities for community. . . . [The individual] can find his own community, a community that will express his freedom, his individual interests, even his eccentricities.[31]

Going even further in his celebration of urban values, Gibson Winter describes his view of urbanization in a book significantly titled *The New Creation as Metropolis*. Pointing to the emergence of the metropolitan area as the characteristically American expression of community, Winter describes metropolis as "the possibility of a unified, human society arising from the chaos of our massive, urban areas."[32] The point of his analysis is that urbanization does not necessarily destroy human values. It may inhibit some traditional forms of human interaction that we have come to cherish, but it also opens up the possibility of new kinds of human community which we are only beginning to realize. These new expressions of community are not inimical to the Christian faith but rather affirm and support it. The role of the church must be to learn and to practice the best of the new ways of metropolis while, at the same time, it stands in judgment against all attempts to limit and fragment the metropolitan community.

Winter had already raised serious questions about the adequacy of the traditional parish for a ministry to such a society. In the openness and interdependence that characterize modern urban society, the local church represents a retreat for the fainthearted who seek out a community in which they can become known and cared for, an artificial version of the traditional small town. Turning away from the larger community of metropolis, they erect for themselves small, homogeneous residential neighborhoods where threatening differences can be kept at bay. The church has based its ministry on this residential neighborhood and, as a result, has allied itself with the most fearful reactionary forces in the city.[33]

Winter's denunciation of the parish has produced some skepticism as to the viability of that venerable institution. At the same time, even admitting its obvious inadequacies, few churchmen have yet shown much willingness to abandon the only form of Christian ministry that is proving stable and self-supporting. The emerging consensus, apparently, is that the parish will have to be supplemented by additional ministries that are more flexible and highly specialized. It is not at all clear that the shortcomings of parish life are so glaring that the church ought to repudiate the significant work that the parish now performs.

This investigation into the nature of urban society and the role of the church in that society is still too new to have borne much fruit. What has emerged so far is an awareness of the possibilities for Christian life and community in urban America. This is a major accomplishment for American Protestantism and a refreshing change from the antiurbanism and antimodernism of the past. At the same time, the Protestant community will have to guard itself against the temptation to accept uncritically all that goes by the name of urban or modern. Hopefully, by making an affirmation of the fundamental worth and value of modern city life, the churches will then be able to evaluate every aspect of that life and to pronounce judgment upon it according to whether it contributes to or militates against the creation of a sound and healthful environment for the best of human community and culture.

8 THE PERSISTENT PERPLEXITY
OF RACE

IT WOULD BE presumptuous to attempt to deal with the complex
and controversial topic of race relations within the limits of a
single brief chapter, but the importance of the issue requires that
it be given some attention. This chapter, therefore, will attempt
to establish three modest assertions about race and religion. First,
the church's views, attitudes, and actions in the matter of race
are based necessarily upon the state of scientific knowledge about
race. Second, the scientific doctrine of the equality of the races
is a fairly recent phenomenon which is only now filtering down
into the cultural consciousness of America and of the church.
Third, the Negro revolution, which has resulted from this new
consciousness of racial equality, has involved the church in a
significant way, but the quality of that involvement cannot yet be
evaluated. In the long run, it will have to be evaluated on the
theological level. Only if the church remains true to its Christian

profession, no matter what the cost, can it make a significant contribution to the ultimate solution of the "Negro question."

During the current racial crisis, the church has frequently been taken to task for its inability or unwillingness to involve itself responsibly in the movement for full equality for the Negro. The church has been castigated as a bulwark of the segregated system, a moral support for anti-Negro attitudes and a betrayer of the Christian cause. While these harsh polemics have their usefulness as a stimulus to action, they inevitably miss the point. They fail to account for the reasons behind the church's willingness to condone segregation. As a result, segregation becomes too easily identified with sinfulness—indeed, it is frequently seen as the only significant social sin—and integration identified with the cause of eternal righteousness.

In discussing the racial question, it is important to begin by recognizing that Christianity does not absolutize any social system or political order. It is not intrinsically monarchical or democratic, capitalist or socialist, slave or free, segregated or integrated. To assert otherwise is to fly in the face of history, for at one time or other thoughtful Christians have, in good conscience, defended every one of these varieties of social order. Any specifically Christian approach to race relations must, therefore, be understood within the context of the culture and the state of the knowledge that it possesses. Politics, psychology, anthropology, and biology have to be taken into consideration. It is not enough to appeal to St. Paul or even to our Lord's own teachings, for the Christian conscience must be informed by disciplines outside the context of faith.

On the basis of this understanding of the effect of cultural change on religious thought, it is possible to distinguish certain events in American history which have enlarged the Christian perception of the proper place of the Negro in society. Each new view of the Negro won acceptance only after a period of struggle in which it was opposed by an older view that claimed the sanction of tradition.

THE PARADOX OF EQUALITY AND INEQUALITY

The first radical change was the introduction of the belief in the equality of all men, a view which stemmed from the French and English Enlightenment. This doctrine was developed consciously to serve as a weapon against the traditional hierarchical social outlook characteristic of Europe in the eighteenth century. Transferred to America, the newer view won ready acceptance because it accorded well with the social facts. Here was no hereditary nobility, no landed aristocracy, no artificial restraints to keep a man from winning his own place in society. The doctrine of equality legitimized the conditions of the present and the hopes of the future. It was only natural, therefore, that the phrase, "all men are created equal" should be enshrined in the Declaration of Independence.

But while the Declaration of Independence marked out an advance in social thought, its implications were only dimly perceived. The American Revolution brought no major shifts in society. After the fighting was over, there were still the customary property restrictions on the right to vote. It took almost another generation to establish the principle of universal male suffrage. Women, of course, were excluded from the privilege of voting. Thus the doctrine of equality did not produce actual political and social equality for all persons.

In this climate of opinion, there was naturally no thought that the equality of all men was shared by the Negro. This exclusion of the Negro from equality was not an oversight, nor was it merely the self-interested racial consciousness of the southern slave holder. It was based on the best scientific thought of the day, the thought of the very Enlightenment that developed the doctrine of equality.

This paradox comes to a focus in the thought of Thomas Jefferson, author of the Declaration of Independence and the leading apostle of the Enlightenment on the American continent.

Jefferson sincerely believed in equality, yet he too accepted the current racial theory that saw the Negro race as inherently inferior. This view was based on the concept that God's creation was perfect and hence unchanging. Since the Negro was then inferior in social status, in the degree of his civilization, and in intellectual attainment, it was concluded that he was inherently inferior. The theory had no place for a doctrine of development, such as the later nineteenth century was to devise.

Jefferson was never satisfied with this quandary. He wanted to believe that equality included all men, yet he could not square this belief with what he took to be the clear evidence of Negro inferiority. He had to admit that, unhappily, there was no choice but to accept Negro inferiority on scientific grounds, much as he would have preferred to extend the boundaries of his belief in equality.[1]

ANTISLAVERY AND INEQUALITY

During the years of the antislavery movement, the belief in the equality of all men continued to be held in an uncomfortable association with the contradictory belief in the inferiority of the Negro. Even the abolitionists and other antislavery men differed in their estimates of the Negro's capabilities. Some were committed to a doctrine of the fundamental equality of whites and Negroes. On the other hand, there were antislavery societies that excluded Negroes from membership. One perceptive writer on the antislavery movement considers that the failure to make full use of the free Negro was one of the chief weaknesses of the movement.[2]

Leading abolitionists often failed to take any action to ensure civil rights for free Negroes in northern states, where they were frequently harassed and commonly denied the right to vote. The numerous colonization schemes that were popular in the earlier days of the antislavery movement were no more than an attempt to abolish the Negro problem by abolishing the Negro from

American society. The Negroes themselves saw through the false humanitarianism of the colonization scheme and protested bitterly against it.

Even though the antislavery movement often shared the racist presuppositions of the rest of American society, it brought to the nation a new concern for the Negro. Within the churches, antislavery men called the churches' teachings and practices into question, brought the slavery issue into the foreground, and insisted upon its discussion. As a result, those churches which contained significant minorities of antislavery crusaders were torn violently apart by the struggle. Slave-holding became a controversial issue for church discipline and the bitterness of the struggle produced splits in the Methodist, Baptist, and Presbyterian denominations.

The slavery controversy illustrates how the church slowly and painfully accommodates to new modes of thinking. When the gap between the old ideas and the new became too wide for Christian fellowship to bridge, the fellowship broke up in a ferment of hostility, defensiveness, and righteous indignation. Contemporary observers can see that the southerners ought to have renounced slavery or that the northerners should not have pressed the issue so vigorously, but such judgments are easily made only from the superior vantage point of time. Given the historical situation, the schisms were probably inevitable, unless the opponents of slavery had blunted their convictions to the point where they would have denied the truth they sincerely believed in. The forces of economics, self-interest, social pressure, and ideological justification were too powerful for the southerners to resist.

SEGREGATION IN THE CHURCHES

In both North and South, meanwhile, convictions about Negro inferiority were producing an institution that was to become a feature of American Protestant church life for the indefinite future—the Negro church.

Negro churches apparently evolved because of the poor treatment given free Negroes in mixed churches. Kyle Haselden lists, among other indignities, "the special partitions and galleries for worshipers of the Negro race; segregation in the time of worship for the different races where the same building had to be used by both," as well as the antagonistic attitudes of official church bodies.[3]

The attitude of the white churches is not hard to understand, given the state of racial theory at the time. The Protestant churches have always prided themselves on the close, personal, familylike atmosphere of the congregation. Since society was agreed that the Negro race was inferior to the white, it was impossible to maintain any genuine mutuality of interpersonal encounter that would make interracial congregational life possible. The best that could be expected would be a sentimental paternalism that accepted the Negro's proximity, but which denied him any chance to exercise either leadership or independence.

So the Negroes gradually withdrew from the mixed congregations and formed their own churches. Sometimes they would found a congregation and then affiliate with a predominantly white denomination. This was the case with St. Thomas' Church in Philadelphia, which was founded as a Negro church and only later affiliated with the Protestant Episcopal Church. New Negro denominations were also formed, notably the African Methodist Episcopal Church.

While the Negro church may be seen as a judgment on the lack of vision of white churches, it served a valuable purpose for the Negro community. Throughout the years of the Negro's cultural isolation, the Negro church served as the focal point of his community life. As Kyle Haselden has expressed it:

It became the school in which Negro leadership was trained and developed; it became his refuge and shelter from the otherwise constant hammerings of an indifferent and hostile white society; it became the source of power, inspiring him toward the full expression of his humanity and undergirding his claims for a full integration in American life with an inflexible conviction of divine approval.[4]

The Union victory in the Civil War brought freedom to the Negro slave, but it marked no great breakthrough in white America's attitude toward the Negro himself. Negroes in the North suffered few legal disabilities, but segregation of Negroes continued by custom. In the South, as C. Vann Woodward points out, segregation began in the churches and the schools during the early days of reconstruction. It was not until around the 1890's, however, that Jim Crow laws were generally adopted to solidify the segregated social order.[5] The process was sanctified by the United States Supreme Court in the case of Plessy *v.* Ferguson in 1896. In that decision, the Court affirmed the constitutionality of segregated facilities for Negroes on the ground that equality did not require racial mixing. This "separate but equal" doctrine permitted the development of a comprehensive system of legalized segregation.

In both North and South, the churches remained almost entirely segregated. The combination of the voluntary principle of church organization and the tradition of congregational independence contributed to the persistence of segregation in church life. Most Protestant churches had no central authority that could require a congregation to minister to all races without distinctions. Moreover, in many denominations the congregation customarily votes on prospective church members. Few Negroes could be expected to risk the humiliation that would come with rejection by an all-white congregation.

But again, this system cannot be attributed purely to human sinfulness. No doubt the sinfulness was there in abundance, but it was supported by the authority of modern science. Late nineteenth-century thought was dominated by the Darwinian conception of development through struggle, competition, and the survival of the fittest. Transposed into the area of racial theory, this version of Darwinism lent support to a view of race that distinguished between the more advanced races and those in lower stages of development. It took little imagination to view the Negro race as an inferior one, while the Anglo-Saxon, who was awarded the status of a separate race in this mode of thinking, was seen as the divinely predestined bearer of Christianity and civilization.

Thus the doctrine of the inherent superiority of the white race was powerfully reinforced by the prestige of modern science. It is possible to discern an equally powerful process of rationalization in the acceptance of this brand of racial theory since it accorded so well with the deepest desires and the strongest interests of its exponents. Certainly the theory failed to convince many educated Negroes. There was also a cadre of white liberals, some of them in the churches, who rejected such ideas as sheer nonsense. Nevertheless, there were many sincere and devout Christians who accepted racist theory on scientific grounds, even though they accounted themselves friends of the Negro.

Christian humanitarians who accepted the doctrine of Negro inferiority were still moved to work for the amelioration of the Negro's plight and to ensure his civil rights. During the years of reconstruction, many northern Christians went into the South to provide educational opportunities for the newly freed Negroes. In later years, education and job-training projects continued to attract the attention of church members. The social gospel movement included "the Negro question" on its agenda for the improvement of American society, although no evidence exists that this concern implied any belief in racial equality. The late nineteenth century continued to display an ambivalent attitude toward the Negro. Outside the South, there was a disposition to accord the Negro equal rights under the law, but at the same time, American society refused to admit him to any measure of personal equality.

THE SCIENTIFIC DEMOLITION OF RACISM

Throughout the entire period, however, some men rejected the doctrine of racial inequality no matter how it was dressed in scientific garb. They represented only a small minority until they were joined by a number of leading scientists. The Darwin-Spencer view of race gradually broke down, to be replaced by the theory that *Homo sapiens* is both genus and species and that, therefore, all the races of mankind share a common origin.[6] This doctrine, based on far-reaching scientific research, was a decisive blow to all theories of racial inequality. Working on the basis of this theory, later anthropologists have come to regard the whole concept of race as essentially meaningless for any systematic understanding of groups of human beings. It has been from the world of science, then, that the final rejection of racial inferiority has emanated.

The implications of this new doctrine are momentous. It means that there is now no good reason for preserving any racial inequalities in society. It means that total integration of society is both desirable and necessary. It means that the words "white" and "Negro," as designations for different kinds of human beings, have no precise, scientific meaning. The door has been opened for a new kind of racial equality, a total equality that reaches into every area of social, economic, and political life.

This change in the anthropological view of race did not have many immediate consequences. It took until the late 1940's for the doctrine to become influential enough to change the actual conditions of society. It was implicitly accepted as the basis for President Harry Truman's executive order which desegregated the Armed Forces in 1948. It underlay the United States Supreme Court's recent rejection of segregation in public educational facilities, both in Justice Fred Vinson's 1950 decision in the case of Sweatt *v.* Painter and in Justice Earl Warren's 1954 decision in the famous case of Brown *v.* Board of Education of Topeka. These decisions established the constitutional principle that segregation by race is prejudicial to the interests of the Negro because it sets him apart from the larger society and induces in him feelings of inferiority. For the first time, the Supreme Court was saying that the Negro was fully equal to the white man, not only as a citizen, but as a person.

The scientific position on race has been one of the chief factors in the current Negro revolution. By now it has permeated most of American society and has made it impossible to defend the traditional patterns of racial segregation. More important, it has permeated the Negro community itself, opening up to the Negro a vision of complete equality in a society free of any racial bias, a society which will afford him both economic opportunity and social acceptance, a society in which he can be merely a human being. It is this hope which has fired the Negro's burst of energy, tenacity, and resourcefulness in breaking down traditional patterns of segregated life.

THE CHURCHES AND THE NEGRO REVOLUTION

During the period we have been discussing, the churches have been involved in the same processes of change as has the rest of American society. Like the United States Supreme Court, the churches have made pronouncements about racial equality throughout the twentieth century. In so doing, the churches have relied upon the conclusions of scientific investigators, just as they must rely upon science to decide whether the world was created in six days or in 8.7 billion years. In this sense, it is no particular disgrace to the church that its doctrine of racial equality did not precede that of the scientists because racial theory is necessarily based on biology and anthropology. The theologian cannot construct a coherent doctrine of race out of a collection of verses from the Bible.

At the same time, the Protestant churches in America are open to the charge of having failed to protest the disgraceful treatment of Negroes in both the North and the South. The churches have done little to relieve the poverty and exploitation from which Negroes have long suffered in America. They have likewise done little to foster mutual contact and communication across racial lines. There is much that the churches could have done in this area, even within the framework of the now outmoded doctrine of racial inferiority.

Be that as it may, the churches today have accepted the newer racial theory with only very minor exceptions. The doctrine of

Negro equality and the consequent Negro revolution have posed two significant questions for the churches. First, what is to be the place of the Negro in the life of the church? Second, what is the role of the church in the Negro's drive to realize his equality in American society? To take the second question first, let us examine the church's part in the current civil rights movement.

There has been considerable complaint that the churches have come into the civil rights movement only in its very late stages. On the other hand, there is some feeling of pride on the part of the churches in what they have already been able to accomplish. Both assertions contain something of the truth. Martin Luther King's Montgomery bus boycott came out of the Negro churches and the lunch counter sit-ins were strongly supported by Negro Christian college students; the white churches got involved in civil rights in a major way only after 1960, by which time the movement had generated its own momentum.

At the same time, it is clear that the successful passage of the Civil Rights Act of 1964 owes something to the participation of the churches in the nationwide drive for enactment. Moral pressure from back home aided in lining up votes from some midwestern congressmen and senators who had no deep commitment to either side of the issue. Much of this moral pressure emanated from the churches. Members were encouraged to write their congressmen. Frequent visits to Washington were arranged for delegates from all over the country. While the effect of these tactics cannot be measured with any precision, there is good ground for claiming that the churches made a valuable contribution to the passage of the Act.

In their relationship to the civil rights movement, the churches have gained as much as they have contributed. For some time, the Protestant churches of America had been feeling themselves to be on the fringes of society. They no longer had the prestige and the influence that they had once enjoyed. They did not participate in the major decisions of the society, nor did they, as we say, "speak to the power structures" of society. They were acutely conscious of being isolated, peripheral, and irrelevant.

The civil rights movement has changed all that. Today the

churches are again in the center of a major social movement. Once more the Protestant lobby is being taken seriously in Washington. Once more the activities of church groups are making headlines apart from the religion page of the newspaper.

Moreover, the civil rights movement is enabling the Protestant churches to make peace with the political and social liberals. It is important to remember that the liberal intelligentsia of America includes a significant proportion of renegade Protestants who have rejected their religious heritage because of its obscurantism, fundamentalism, anti-intellectualism, and social conservatism. The civil rights movement is bringing them into contact with another kind of Protestantism, a Protestantism that is intellectually alive and socially concerned. The results of this contact can be only beneficial for both the churches and the secular intellectuals.

The new Protestant involvement in social action has been especially exhilarating for the ministers, who have been the particular victims of the churches' sense of estrangement from the mainstream of society. The minister is being given another chance to assert his moral leadership. He can feel himself to be performing a useful social function. This factor is especially important inasmuch as many clergy had begun to wonder if they really had a function in modern secular society. Perhaps this feeling of suddenly finding oneself useful may explain the extraordinary fervor with which some of the younger clergy have thrown themselves into the civil rights movement.

THE NEW MORALISM OF CIVIL RIGHTS

The participation of the churches in the civil rights movement has not been without its costs. To be sure, some conservatives have withdrawn their support from their churches and some outspoken clergymen have lost their jobs. But such events as these are not serious for the churches. They are only the inevitable hardships accompanying any movement that has force and direc-

tion. Indeed, they may help the Protestant churches to develop a
new sense of their own integrity, a sense that has been notably
lacking in the past.

The cost of which I speak is, rather, a regrettable lapse into
a new moralistic absolutism. Since the Negro revolution began,
the whole question of Negro rights has been interpreted rather
consistently in moral terms, untempered by much sensitivity to
the ambiguities of history. As a result, the movement has shown
little patience with differences and little tolerance for criticism,
even of a friendly sort. The moralistic equation of integration
with the Good and segregation with Evil has the merit of simplicity, but it does violence to the facts. Certainly there is a clear
and compelling moral imperative in the Negro's search for his
rightful place in American society. The difficulty comes when
integration becomes an absolute and the civil rights movement
becomes a moral crusade.

The crusading spirit produces two unfortunate results. The first
and most obvious is the harsh and judgmental attitude it engenders with respect to the opposition. In spite of the considerable
rhetoric about the need to love one's enemies, the movement
tends to condemn all opposition. Judgment is pronounced not
only against diehard white supremacists but also against moderates who may oppose a specific tactic or objective. Negroes who
counsel moderation are easily written off as "Uncle Toms" whose
arguments deserve no answer. Lately, even the "white liberal"
has come in for his share of scorn. Activist clergy are prone to
read their more cautious colleagues out of the church. Civil rights
enthusiasts have shown much impatience with any attempt to understand, to conciliate, to compromise, or to reconcile. Such suggestions are considered cowardly and half-hearted.

This is a curious attitude to come out of a generation that
has presumably been raised on Reinhold Niebuhr. It represents
a step backward into the era of ideology, the era in which Christian moral crusaders were sure that they had the right answers
for society and were quite uninterested in the complexities of
social analysis and the ambiguities of politics.

The second unfortunate result of moral absolutism is the tendency to excuse and justify any and all tactics useful in the cause. The danger in this tendency has been materially reduced by the firm commitment of the southern Negroes to nonviolent tactics. Peaceful demonstrations, even those in technical violation of the law, are not too hard to justify, especially when the extremists in the opposition are resorting to terrorism and murder. Justification becomes more difficult when the tactic is a mass sit-in that brings government or business to a grinding halt. The actions of some chapters of the Congress of Racial Equality in northern cities in stopping traffic and boycotting the schools have been similarly questionable. Martin Luther King's regrettable threat to boycott the entire state of Alabama was even more dubious.

To be sure, any movement that contains vitality and a sense of urgency is likely to engage in some questionable tactics. That is understandable. Still, there has been too little disposition to make the necessary distinctions between those tactics that are justifiable and those that are not. The prophetic voice in the civil rights movement has rarely been directed to the movement itself.

The usual explanation for this fact is that the civil rights movement must present a united front. Any hint of internal dissension weakens the movement by giving aid and comfort to the enemy. This is the same argument that is used by supporters of American foreign policy, "no matter what." Any critic of any policy can be effectively silenced by pointing out the danger of dissension in the face of the enemy.

The conviction that the morality of the cause justifies any tactic is a natural outgrowth of the attitude of moral absolutism. So too is the inability to handle friendly criticism. The danger to the civil rights movement in this tendency to ideological rigidity is obvious. It can only lead to the kind of splintering that has hampered the efforts of nearly every radical social or political movement in recent history.

It is the careful concentration on the morality of means that has given the civil rights movement its overwhelming moral authority in America, cutting the ground from under its most extreme opponents. Should that authority be lost by the adoption of revolutionary tactics, the extremists in the opposition would be encouraged and the support of the general public would be forfeited. The best hope for the future is the emergence of a moderate consensus that will embrace both races in both North and South. That consensus can hardly begin to develop so long as "moderate" remains a dirty word.

THE NEGRO MINISTER

The participation of the churches in the civil rights movement can best be seen as it comes to a focus in the role of the clergyman. To see this role with any clarity, it will be necessary to examine the white and Negro clergy separately, since they play quite different parts in the movement. Each has his own special opportunities and each works under his own peculiar set of pressures.

Clearly the Negro clergyman has been the spearhead of the Negro revolution. This is no accident for, as we have seen, the Negro church has long been the leading Negro social institution and the breeding ground for Negro leadership. The Negro minister's leadership of the civil rights movement has been impressive and beneficial. It has given the movement a fundamental Christian moral flavor and a consistent sense of restraint and good humor which is infectious and attractive. Even at his most militant, the Negro clergyman is essentially moderate in his goals and his methods.

At the moment, the Negro minister is enjoying the luxury of leading a moral crusade against injustice and at the same time leading his own people toward a goal which they all desire: freedom, equality, and economic and social betterment. His crisis lies in the future, perhaps in the not too distant future. Now that the civil rights drive is over the top, there is a possibility that leadership may pass into the hands of a newly emerging type: the hard-boiled Negro politician who is more concerned with "our rights" than with the niceties of nonviolent moderation.

The political Negro can use the same moral arguments that the ministers use, but he can also appeal more directly to the impatience, the frustration, the hostility, and the resentment which many Negroes feel at the slow pace of integration. He can provide more dramatic leadership. He can promise to move faster and farther. In short, he will soon offer a significant challenge to the leadership of the patient and moderate Negro clergyman.

What will the Negro clergy do then? Their prophetic role will be to fight to maintain the restraint and moderation that has so far characterized the Negro's struggle. But to do that, the minister will have to swim against the current and it may be a very strong current. He will constantly be tempted to become a professional Negro and to outshout the politicians. In other words, his Christian profession is likely to pull him in one direction, his Negro profession in another.

Negro clergy frequently express concern about the matter. Their dilemma is that, if they say, "Slow down," they may be labeled as "Uncle Toms" and their influence will be lost. Yet as Christian ministers, the day may soon come when they will be called upon to say, "Slow down."

However the dilemma is resolved, the Negro church will be judged in the event. In that day, we will learn whether the Negro church will succeed at the point where most of white Protestantism has consistently failed. Has the Negro church produced a fundamental Christian orientation that can act as a leaven in society, to shape and direct a powerful social movement? Or will it prove to be merely another variety of culture religion that supports the social and political attitudes of its members?

The test lies ahead. Its outcome may determine the success or failure of the Negro's search for equality in America. If the politicians win and the Negro Christians decide to be Negroes first and Christians second, then their efforts will produce not true equality but a lasting social schism. If their Christian commitment transcends their racial consciousness, we may be well on the way toward building a genuinely interracial society in America.

THE WHITE MINISTER

The white clergyman works under a quite different set of pressures. Within the civil rights movement he occupies a subordinate position, since the leadership of the movement devolves primarily upon Negroes. He is called upon to participate in demonstrations, to mobilize community opinion, and to sit on interracial boards and commissions.

His strategic importance lies in his continuous communication with the more conservative elements in his community. His chief task, therefore, is to extend the moderate consensus, to spread the conviction that Negroes are equal to whites and that they deserve completely equal treatment. In the final analysis, the Negro revolution will succeed only as it achieves the tacit support of the conservative sector of American society. There is no good reason why this should not be given. Conservative business leaders desire the maintenance of social order and stability. Racial conflicts are inimical to sound labor relations. Industrial expansion depends upon social harmony. For all of these reasons, there is every expectation that, as the Negro revolution accomplishes its objectives, the revolutionary fervor will die down and the conservative will come to see that happy, prosperous Negroes are more conducive to social stability than are angry, exploited Negroes.

The white minister can help the conservative to reach this new awareness. In order to do so, however, he must remain in contact with that segment of the community. The clergyman who has real convictions about racial equality, therefore, will be required to walk a tightrope between his civil rights colleagues and his conservative parishioners. If he loses touch with either element, he loses his effectiveness. If he keeps in touch with both, he is likely to be regarded with some suspicion, since both groups will see him as one who does business with the enemy.

Needless to say, this analysis applies with special force to the white Protestant minister in the South. Indeed, it is the awareness of this peculiar vocation that has inhibited the southern clergyman from making any public commitment to the civil rights movement. He can exercise his function of prophecy only once. After that, he passes from the ranks of the prophets into the ranks of the martyrs. Many clergymen have done this and their witness has been noble and courageous. Nevertheless, there are many more who have painfully maintained public silence while working quietly within their communities to promote long-range possibilities for the reconciliation of the races. To maintain their contact with segregationist parishioners, they must keep silent on the issues of the day. Their decision to do so will be vindicated by their long-run accomplishments. If they are able to open up channels for interracial communication and co-operation in the South in the years to come, then their present silence will have been justified.

Both white and Negro clergymen are inescapably involved in the movement for the realization of racial equality. Each labors under his own set of pressures and each is exposed to his own temptations. Both have, as do their parishioners, a major role to play in the development of a truly interracial society. If that should come to pass, then Protestant Christianity, regardless of its color, will have made a significant contribution to American life.

TOWARD AN INTERRACIAL CHURCH

What has been the effect of the doctrine of racial equality on the life of the churches? What is its effect likely to be in the future?

Though nearly every church today accepts the doctrine of racial equality, the churches have the same problems in enforcing their views among their members as the United States Supreme Court has had in enforcing its prohibition of segregation in the public schools. With all the coercive power of the federal government behind it, the Supreme Court has so far succeeded in bringing about integration in only a small percentage of the public schools in the South. Is it any wonder that the churches have fared no better?

Both the church and the federal government are running counter to the accumulated prejudices of generations. Not all southern segregationists are racial bigots and hatemongers. There are thousands of thoughtful and sensitive white Christians who, throughout their lives, have been taught—with the apparent support of what science they have known—that the Negro is inferior and that his development could best take place if he were kept separate from white society. Now, suddenly, both their church and their national government tell them that this view is false. Naturally their inherited beliefs and attitudes lead them to rebel against this new teaching. Their vested interest in the present social system reinforces their rebellion. Their emotional rejection of integration is further encouraged by vicious and unscrupulous state and local politicians who exploit their fears and antagonisms in their own interests.

As a result of these stresses and tensions, the church—in the South and elsewhere—has entered one of those regrettable periods of cultural lag in which the contradictions in her own life and thought are simply too great for accommodation. It seems clear that, on this matter of the place of the Negro in American society, the church will continue to be divided against itself for some time to come.

As the church begins to adjust to the new climate of race relations, it is possible to observe on a grand scale the processes by which the church adapts to social change. An advance guard, composed of both Negroes and white men, has been in the forefront of the racial revolution, completely convinced of its fundamental righteousness. They provide the agitation that brings the issue to the consciousness of the church and of the society as a whole. The most hopeful sign in this development is that many of the most responsible officials of the major churches have espoused advanced positions on civil rights and Negro equality. A large portion of the urban clergy have committed themselves to the movement and many devout laymen have been active as well. In the past, most reforms have been accomplished from the fringes of the church acting upon a recalcitrant center. This reform seems to be proceeding from the very center of the church's life.

At present, the church is feeling the effects of cultural lag most painfully. In the North, where the integration of society has progressed furthest, the church may still be the most segregated institution in existence. This condition will not be easy to cure. What, for example, is to be done about the Negro denomination? It has its own power structure as well as its own tradition and heritage. It has had great value in the life of the Negro subculture. Has integration proceeded so far as to make the Negro church obsolete? Most observers think not. So long as the white churches remain segregated in spirit, the Negro church will have to remain in existence. Perhaps the greatest need in the ecumenical movement in America is for a greater degree of interaction between the white churches and the Negro churches. Out of this process may come a greater willingness on both sides to join forces in a genuinely interracial expression of the Christian life.

The separate organization of Negro life within predominantly white denominations represents no less a problem. In the Methodist merger of 1939, Negro congregations were segregated into a Central Jurisdiction as a concession to the South. The General Conference of the Methodist Church has recently provided for the elimination of the Central Jurisdiction and the gradual absorption of its constituent congregations into the regular Conferences.

This step represents an advance, but still it integrates only the official church councils. The nub of the problem is the local congregation. In spite of the advance of the civil rights movement, in spite of the advance in white Protestant thinking and action with respect to the Negro, it must still be conceded that there are few stable integrated congregations in American Protestantism today. Occasionally a few Negro families will be found in a white congregation or a few whites will be found attending a Negro church. More frequently, an integrated congregation is merely a temporary phenomenon in an area where the racial composition of the population is changing. Within the congregations, there is still much passive resistance to any change in existing racial patterns of church membership.

It is hard to interest churchmen in this problem because there seems to be little urgency about the matter. Most local congregations are still neighborhood churches, drawing their membership from a relatively small area. Since residential patterns in America are almost completely segregated along racial lines, there is little impetus to congregational integration. "We have no Negroes in our neighborhood," is a frequent response when the question of racial integration is raised. Congregations who see no immediate problem in their own neighborhood are understandably reluctant to go out of their way to raise the question.

For the foreseeable future, then, continued agitation will be necessary to ensure that the church continues to move toward the goal of complete integration of its life. It remains to be determined just what form the agitation should take.

The most pressing need is to increase the interracial character of the local congregation. For some time now, white churches have been encouraging Negroes to join them, particularly in areas where Negroes are moving in for the first time. While this approach is a necessary minimum, it puts all of the stress on the Negro. Perhaps we have reached the point where white parishioners should be encouraged to join Negro congregations with Negro clergy, thus taking upon themselves the demand to risk humiliation and nonacceptance. Granted this tactic is highly artificial, but so is the segregated neighborhood. And I suspect that it is easier to change one's parish affiliation than to change one's neighborhood.

It is also necessary to expand the small attempts that have already been made to integrate the church's ministry. Negro clergy too often constitute an ecclesiastical subculture. They are available only for work in Negro congregations or as assistants to white pastors in areas that are becoming Negro. Certainly team ministries could easily be integrated. Negro pastors ought to be encouraged to employ white assistants. White congregations ought to be urged to consider candidates for vacancies regardless of race. While these steps are in process, the churches could employ various stratagems to help white parishioners get used to the idea that Negroes are numbered among their clergy. Pulpit exchanges can be helpful. Integration of the staffs of youth conferences, summer camps, and official church organizations would be even more useful. In all of these ways, church members can be taught that every minister is ordained for service in the whole church.

Since the segregated neighborhood is the basis of the segregated congregation, Christians have a special obligation to work for open housing in whatever ways are available. This is a more difficult and less glamorous aspect of the drive for integration. It calls not for freedom marches and rallies, but for patient and determined work behind the scenes. Since it poses a genuine threat to the old ways of society, it also promises a collision with the most demonic forces in the community: the power of property and profits.

THE PARTICULAR PERPLEXITIES OF THE SOUTH

Most of these suggestions apply particularly to the North, but the same principles apply to the South. The immediate situation in the South is different, of course, because the threat to traditional values and practices is far greater. The religious crisis is more serious for the southerner as well. For generations he has been told that God created the separate races and that God intended to keep them separate. He learned to integrate this teaching into his understanding of the Christian faith. Now suddenly, and apparently at the instigation of the United States Supreme Court, he is told that the old doctrine is false and that the southern way of life is a fraud. He is told, further, that he will have to admit the Negro into full equality in his social system. Finally, he is told that he must rethink his Christian convictions in the light of this new information.

This startling change poses no particular problem for those who are convinced segregationists first and Christians second. It is easy enough for men to choose only those doctrines that fit their secular interests. Opportunists have been doing that for centuries. But it produces a real crisis of conscience for those Christians who are genuinely concerned to make sense out of this overturning of their long-cherished convictions. With the best will in the world, resistance is inevitable in such a situation. Inevitable too is the deep-seated feeling of resentment against those who have brought the crisis about: Negroes and northern agitators.

The division of white and Negro Christians in the South is related to the issue of social change. Typically the white Christian is on the side of order and he is likely to interpret his Christianity as a stabilizing force in society, which it is in fact. The Negro Christian is typically on the side of change and he is prone to interpret his Christianity as a force for revolution, which it is as well. For each, self-interest adds urgency to what is already his proclivity. The result is provocation on one side and resistance on the other; impatience on the part of the Negro and anxiety on the part of the white.

Just as there is a major cultural lag in the North, there is a similar lag in the South. Just as the northern lag keeps northern white Christians from seeking out opportunities for involvement with their Negro brethren, so the lag in the South keeps southern white Christians from welcoming the coming changes in the relationship between the races. Southerners have traditionally shown a great deal of affection for Negroes so long as they "kept their place." Today they are called to face radical changes in the nature of that place.

Perhaps the most significant task for the church in the South is to help in keeping open some of the old channels of communication between the races. In this task, Christians can perform a distinguished service for the entire community, for Christians already have channels open to them and a basis of shared convictions that go beyond the externals of shared citizenship.

If past experience with cultural lags is any indication, this process of change will be painful if not tragic. Time and again in the past, the church has been split and fragmented by the pressures that result when the social gaps are too wide to be easily closed. It is too soon to tell how deeply the churches are split over the issue of race, but there is no doubt that the new teachings are making headway in both North and South, in spite of the resistance of tradition and self-interest.

If this analysis has any point to make, it is that accusations concerning the church's failure to come to terms with the racial crisis are essentially meaningless, regardless of the truth in what they have to say. Certainly by today's standards, the performance of American Protestantism in the area of race relations has been poor. In this respect, our age is hardly in a position to judge the past too harshly. Every age must act in the light of its own best knowledge. Our knowledge of the Negro has undergone radical revision at the hands of the social and biological scientists. That is the task of the scientist. The task of the church is to put this knowledge to use for the benefit of all men. In doing so, it is inevitably required to fight against its own best knowledge of past ages. Thus the church finds itself at odds with itself and only time and agitation can bring the new knowledge to bear fruit in new forms of life, in the society, and in the church itself.

9 SOME HOPEFUL THOUGHTS ON AN
UNCERTAIN FUTURE

IT IS DIFFICULT to find patterns of order and consistency in a work which is devoted to the description of variety and movement. Our purpose has been to identify a creative edge in American Protestantism and to show how it has affected the Protestant outlook in several major areas of social life. This creative segment of Protestantism has come to grips with new problems courageously and resourcefully and has sought new solutions. In doing so, it has absorbed new information and, as a result, has developed new attitudes and viewpoints which enable Protestant Christianity to adjust to new social conditions.

Progressive Protestantism has constituted only a small minority of the whole church, but it has provided most of the movement that has been described. It has occupied the advance positions which have only gradually become part of the over-all Protestant consensus. Today the advance positions of progressive Protestantism are still far ahead of the bulk of the denominations.

This process of movement and change has been partly responsible for the incredible variety in American Protestantism. Old positions never die, apparently; they merely stay around to add to the confusion. As new ideas become accepted and new positions taken, the old abandoned ones still appeal to enough people, for one reason or another, to enable them to stay alive indefinitely. Thus every new development adds another variation to the already excessive diversity of American Protestantism. I offer no cure for this regrettable phenomenon. I merely mention it to justify the fact that, no matter what has been said here about the changing position of the church on any issue, the contrary could be maintained with equal veracity.

THE DIRECTION OF CHANGE

In the changes that American Protestantism has undergone, it is possible to detect a fairly consistent direction. In earlier times, churchmen seemed to be preoccupied primarily with their own institutional goals and purposes. In facing a social or political question, they were likely to ask, "How can the church's interests best be served?" Whether the matter was Sabbatarian legislation, or the privileged position occupied by religion in the schools, or the denominational competition for control of the colleges, Protestant action in the public realm tended to be governed largely by considerations of institutional self-seeking.

This early emphasis on self-interest gradually gave way to a larger concern for shaping the society in a Christian mold, as Protestantism understood it. The churches became interested in political morality, in organized charities, in Christianizing the social order. This attitude contained a high ethical impulse and a genuine solicitude for human welfare. Yet it also harbored a possessive attitude toward the nation which was conceived to be

"Protestant America." Correspondingly, it regarded with suspicion the "foreign" elements, by which was meant Roman Catholic and Jewish. It tended to be moralistic and theologically imperialistic. It knew what was good for people and its conception of what was good was colored by the small-town bourgeois mentality of the typical American Protestant.

Time and new social conditions have modified and reshaped this attitude. The Protestant social outlook is only now beginning to adjust to the new conditions of contemporary American society. This new outlook involves the acceptance of a minority status in a secularized society which contains a great variety of religious groups. It is too soon yet for most Protestants to be quite aware of their new situation or to understand its implications. Some preliminary observations may, however, be in order.

This new social order is secular. That is to say, the various spheres of life which formerly were fitted into a theological framework have declared their independence and now justify themselves on the basis of their own inner logic. Politics, art, music, literature, education, and the various learned disciplines no longer concede any special standing to the theological enterprise. Religion is seldom uppermost in the mind of modern man.

The new social order is religiously pluralistic. American society today contains a wide variety of religious traditions, beliefs, and attitudes. These would include Judaism, Catholicism, Eastern Orthodoxy, and assorted types of Protestantism. But other, less obvious religious outlooks are also represented: humanism, both religious and secular; agnosticism (which is not the same thing); and frank unbelief. The fragmented character of the American religious community exaggerates the apparent predominance of secular modes of thought and action. Actually, there is probably more active religious concern in America today than is commonly supposed.

The new social order is urban in character. Its center of gravity is the city. The city provides the intellectual focus of the society just as it houses its major institutions. The base of the new order is a highly complex industrial establishment made possible by the accomplishments of modern science. The resulting society is characterized by large-scale institutional life with its specialization, interdependence, mobility, and impersonality.

Protestantism's typical reaction to the new order has been negative. The churches, by and large, have stood against progress —except where they have embraced it with uncritical enthusiasm. They have stood against the city and for the small town; against industry and for small farming and craftsmanship; against the university and for the small college; against internationalism and for national aggrandizement; against the complex and for the simple.

Protestant thinkers today are beginning to affirm the new order while they try to make theological sense out of it. They point out that industrialism, urbanization, and secularization contain promise for the future of man as well as threats to what he has long held dear. They see possibilities unfolding for a new kind of life which makes creative use of affluence, leisure, and mass culture. There is a danger in this new attitude that contemporary Protestantism may repeat the tragic errors of the nineteenth-century celebrators of industrial progress, who hailed the benefits of big business while ignoring the terrible human costs of the gilded age. The theologians will have to guard against the temptation to become apologists for dehumanization in their enthusiasm to see what is best in the new society. The social order contains both threat and promise. It is the task of the theologian to help us distinguish between them.

THE SOCIAL TASK OF THE CHURCH

The church's social mission operates on two separate levels. On one level, the church helps men to understand their social and historical situation in order that they may discover how to lead meaningful and responsible lives. At the same time, the church assists the forces of change that are working to reshape the social order so that it may provide a better environment for the human enterprise. The church's ministry on these two levels sometimes brings it into conflict with itself. There is always some tension between the pastors who are concerned with the first level and the prophets whose energies are directed to the second. The pastor often sees the prophet as a shrill and irresponsible disturber of the peace, while the prophet scorns the pastor for his tendency to put spiritual band-aids on the cancers of society.

The church's attitude toward the social order, then, is inevitably both critical and supportive. The church is always required to contend against the exploitation of man by man. It must point to the misuses and abuses of power. It must call attention to the errors, the malice, and the blindness of politicians, educators, managers, and other social leaders. As the interdependence of society increases, holders of power tend to support other holders of power in return for their approval. The critical voice in the society thus becomes muted—in the press, in radio and television, and even in the university. When this happens, the church can ill afford to lower its own prophetic voice, although the gadfly is never very popular.

For its criticism to be valid and useful, the church must at the same time affirm the basic worth and validity of the social order itself. If the church can see no redemptive aspects in the culture, it will become petty and misanthropic. The purpose of prophetic criticism is to help the society to maintain its proper direction, not to destroy its confidence.

The church has, therefore, an obligation to look for ways in which the most vital processes of the society can minister to the deepest needs of mankind. The development of the economy, for example, holds out the promise of both affluence and leisure for most of our population. This has enormous implications for Christian ethics which are now based on an acceptance of the value of work and a suspicion of wasted time. The task of the theologian is not to condemn affluence or leisure, but to discover ways in which they can help to make life richer and more creative so that men do not become enslaved by their new freedom.

THE ALLIANCE WITH LEARNING

It should be clear by now that Protestant thought in the future cannot function in a vacuum, nor can it rely exclusively on its own resources. In this highly specialized civilization, the theologian needs information of many kinds. He needs the insights of the economist, the psychologist, the sociologist, the historian, and all the rest of the scholarly world in order to understand the nature of his society and the ways that it impinges upon his thought. The realization of this need has already begun to dawn upon Protestant thinkers, who have begun to respond by developing new relations with the world of scholarship. This new relationship will hopefully grow into a working alliance of faith and learning, to their mutual benefit. No theologian in the future can dare to make theological pronouncements on social, economic, or political issues without assimilating an impressive amount of technical information.

The partnership of technical knowledge and theological analysis suggests one possible division of labor between clergy and laity. Laymen are the technical experts, the managers, the operators of modern society. They have the knowledge and experience that are required for any judgment of social issues. By working together, the theologian and the lay specialist may be able to develop theological statements that make sense to both of them. Interaction of this sort may prove to be more valuable than the numerous current attempts to make technicians and administrators out of theologically trained clergy while trying to interest working laymen in technical theology.

ECCLESIASTICAL FELLOW TRAVELING

As the church attempts to apply its theological insight to social questions, it will inevitably find it necessary to develop co-operation across the lines of denominations and religious traditions. This process has long been under way, of course. It was characteristic of the social gospel movement. It will no doubt be increased and extended in the future. No denomination has a patent on any of the possible ways of relating faith to social concerns. There is no Presbyterian or Episcopalian way of dealing with a social issue, despite denominational propaganda to the contrary. The issues insist on cutting across the lines. Likewise, the expertise that must be sought is not likely to be found in any one denomination. This situation promises to produce a functional ecumenicity that is far more significant than organic church union, which too often amounts to little more than a merger of ecclesiastical bureaucracies. Such a functional ecumenicity has already begun to appear in urban work, in the campus ministry, and in the civil rights movement. We can expect to see more of it in the future.

There is a further need for co-operation with Catholic, Jewish, and secular forces, organizations, and people. In social action, if the churches are working for some end that promises genuine benefits for all society, they can confidently anticipate that there will be secular groups working toward the same end. There is no social issue to which Catholics, Jews, and secular humanitarians cannot make significant contribution. Any movement that is likely to affect the whole society requires their support and co-operation, for they form a part of the society. Indeed, if a given movement is unable to attract some measure of support from such groups, it is probably not worth considering.

Protestants need to develop a strategy of fellow traveling. At its best, this means the co-operation of various groups in the pursuit of commonly desired ends, in spite of their differences in other areas. The civil rights movement, for example, has been a temporary alliance of churches, labor organizations, liberal politicians, and Negro organizations. The alliance will probably fall apart as the major aims are achieved and the constituent organizations will once again pursue their separate goals. The alliance has had value primarily for this time and for this purpose. There may, of course, be some carry-over into the next project. Men and women who have worked together on something they regard as important will not readily abandon the closeness and camaraderie they have once shared.

This sort of co-operation is quite possible—even necessary—in spite of wide differences in basic beliefs and attitudes. In the common enterprise, it is not often necessary to inquire into those differences, except as they inhibit mutual action. At the same time, the spirit of co-operation creates a climate of trust and confidence in which it is sometimes possible to probe into those differences. Modern secularists are often quite willing to engage in a significant level of dialogue, so long as the Christians do not enter into it with a presumption of their own moral or ideological superiority.

REDEEMING THE INSTITUTIONAL CHURCH

Socially oriented thinking and action must be entered into not just by Christian people but by the churches themselves. Secular society especially needs the corporate witness of the Christian community in the social arena. This means official, organized participation by the churches in social action, planning, and thinking. That is the only way in which the secular society will ever get the message that the churches are concerned and involved as a direct outgrowth of their commitment to the gospel of Christ.

Again the civil rights movement affords an illustration of this. The criticism is often made that the churches entered very late into the civil rights struggle. Exactly what does that mean? In the deepest theological sense, the churches were present all along, for there were concerned and dedicated churchmen involved in the movement from the very beginning. Many of them were involved because of their Christian convictions.

Somehow this message never came across. Any Christian in

the movement could be considered as an exception, an odd variety of unorthodox churchman. It was only when official church bodies issued proclamations, organized commissions on Religion and Race, assigned staff workers to the movement, appropriated funds to help the cause, and employed the vast communications media of the denominations in an effort to arouse the Christian conscience that those outside the church—and many of those inside as well—began to be aware that the church was, indeed, concerned about civil rights for Negroes.

Perhaps this experience can teach the churches a lesson. Our recent preoccupation with the "church in dispersion" has led us into a serious oversimplification of the function of the organized church in society. We have somehow assumed that the "gathered church," the worshiping community, was merely a spiritual service station for the benefit of the members, while the real work of Christ in the world was to be discharged by isolated individual Christians. This point of view downgrades the institution and makes of it an encumbrance to the Christian life.

In this age of institutionalized society, it would be fatally irresponsible for the church to underestimate the usefulness of its own institutional apparatus. So long as most men are accustomed to think of the ecclesiastical institution as The Church, then we can at least make certain that the ecclesiastical organization does work that befits its name.

The responsible use of the ecclesiastical institution is important for another reason. We live in an age in which the institution is the characteristic mode of man's corporate existence. Men commonly work in and act through institutions whether they like it or not. The institution itself can enslave men or it can set them free. We have not yet learned how to construct and operate our institutions so that they contribute to man's freedom rather than to his destruction. Perhaps the best service that the churches could render to the rest of society would be to provide models of creative and responsible institutional life from which the whole society might learn.

This emphasis on the institution as the bearer of Christian

social witness does not imply that Christians can be involved in social action only through their church. On the contrary, Christians ought to be active in the work of every socially useful secular organization. Indeed, there are some areas of society where the most effective Christian involvement can be made only by individuals. Secular institutions such as schools, businesses, labor unions, and industries need the leaven of perceptive and enlightened Christians, and yet the official church bodies are likely to do as much harm as good by attempting to effect any form of institutional penetration. In such situations, the involvement of individual Christians is crucial.

At the same time, more of these dedicated and socially aware Christians ought to become involved in their church organizations. This is risky business, for they stand in danger of becoming casualties of the ushers' guild or the bazaar workshop. If they can survive these hazards, they stand to gain in theological perspective. They may also be able to help the church to strengthen its own social witness. If all interested, dedicated, competent, and aggressive humanitarians leave the church, there will be no one left but the tame, the dull, and the apathetic—and the churches will continue to appear conservative and unimaginative. The churches have labored under this difficulty for too long. It is time for them to call for help, to bring back into the fellowship those who can help to strengthen and sharpen their witness to the society.

As the churches look for ways to increase the significance of their corporate social witness, probably they will find themselves relying more and more upon their clergy, in spite of the current emphasis on the ministry of the laity. In a secular society, the clergy serve as the symbol of the organized church. To the average citizen, the minister *is* the church. If he is active in a movement or fighting for a cause, then the church is *ipso facto* involved.

Aside from his symbolic role, the minister expresses the concern of the church in more concrete ways. The fact that a church is willing to pay the salary of a minister just to work on a university campus or in a civil rights organization means something to those with whom he comes in contact. He is there, not merely as an interested Christian, but as a professional Christian worker, a representative of the ecclesiastical institution. Similarly, when a church official makes a public statement about a political controversy, his voice is heard as the voice of the church. The very same statement could be made by a layman for exactly the same reasons, but it would be attributed to him either in his professional capacity or in his capacity as a private citizen. His theological perspective would probably go unnoticed. This is one of the obvious facts of social life in America today. Rather than complain about it, as is often done, the churches ought to make good use of it.

THE NEED FOR CHURCH DISCIPLINE

The social witness of the Protestant churches, which today is still little more than the private enthusiasm of a small band of zealots, needs to be reinforced by the recovery of a sense of corporate discipline in the life of the church. The excessive individualism of American Protestantism has gradually eroded church discipline to the point where even the traditional beliefs and practices most specifically associated with the several communions have become quite meaningless to the bulk of the membership. As a result, the numerous declarations and pronouncements on social issues that are made by official church bodies produce almost no discernible effect upon the congregations.

The process of recovering church discipline is easier to state than to set in motion. American Protestants are not likely, after all these years, to express a sudden passion for authority in the church. Besides, much of the traditional discipline has been lost because it had no bearing on the conditions of modern life. It appears, then, that one of the church's major tasks in the years ahead will be the formulation of new and meaningful patterns of church discipline. Needless to say, a massive effort will then be required to secure the acceptance of the discipline by the congregations. Only as this aim is achieved will the best of the church's social thought be able to permeate the entire body of believers. Only then might it be anticipated that Christian thought might lead to corresponding Christian action.

One of the most significant aspects of church discipline is that of Christian belief. Throughout this discussion, the church has been treated primarily as a social institution with a set of social functions, a procedure that seems appropriate to an analysis of the interrelations of church and society. It would be a mistake, however, to assume that this is an adequate way of understanding or evaluating the Christian church. The church's contribution to society stands or falls with the theology that it rests upon. While theology lies outside the purview of this discussion, it is not irrelevant to it.

Many of the church's social functions can be subsumed under the heading of "social service" and "social action." But if the church ever becomes merely a social agency, it will soon cease to be even that. The church has a divine mission to proclaim the gospel of Jesus Christ, the Son of God, who was raised from the dead for the salvation of all men. It is because of this saving act of God in history that Christians are impelled into the business of helping their neighbors. It is because God calls men to his service that Christians enter into the service of their society.

Christians who understand their theological grounding can cooperate with secularists and others in the social sphere, not because they are indifferent about beliefs, but because they believe that Christ is Lord of all men, even those who do not believe in him. Because they believe in the universal rule of Christ for the sake of all men, Christians can affirm and support all human striving to make the world more fit for human habitation.

The greatest weakness of the progressive segment of Protestantism is that, historically, it has lacked this theological depth. The tendency in Protestantism has been to emphasize theology *or* secular learning, worship *or* social action. We are only now learning that these facets of the Christian life cannot be separated without a loss of vitality and direction.

The current theological renaissance, therefore, is especially encouraging, as is the accompanying liturgical revival. The two movements together can increase the church's sense of its own integrity and deepen its theological roots. Theology and worship become particularly important in a secular age in which Christians are likely to lose any sense of their distinctiveness because their external conditions closely resemble those of their secular neighbors. If the church is to enter boldly and fully into the whirl and flux of the secular order, it will need firm roots in its own heritage—it must be "like a tree planted by the water," as the Psalm says. Otherwise, the fear of total assimilation into the secular culture may lead the Protestant churches into a panicked withdrawal to an ecclesiastical ghetto where they can hope to ride out the storms of secularism.

The danger is greatest, of course, for the creative edge of Protestantism—for that is the segment of the Protestant community most involved in the secular society and most susceptible to dissolution. The alert, sensitive, intelligent Christian liberal may feel that he has much more in common with the alert, sensitive, intelligent secularists with whom he lives and works than he has with dull, stodgy, conservative Christians with whom he goes to church. The danger of total assimilation can be avoided only by the cultivation of a greater theological awareness and by the conscientious maintenance of institutional loyalty and responsibility. A secular society holds no dangers for a church that is firmly grounded in theology, perceptive about the realities of social life, and committed to an intelligent sense of discipline among its members.

OUTLOOK FOR THE FUTURE

The position of Protestantism in contemporary America is neither stable nor assured. This account of it may seem overoptimistic because we have concentrated on the growing and creative edge. The timid, the sentimental, the reactionary, and the anti-intellectual are still with us. But can we believe that they will dominate the Protestantism of the future?

The social situation of American Protestantism today is potentially almost ideal. There is still enough kindly disposition toward the religious enterprise to make the church at home in the land. At the same time, the increasing secularization of the culture has loosened the bonds of informal establishment to the point where the churches can dare to be critical and creative. Protestantism still has an open door into the conservative sectors of society. It has now begun to develop good relationships in those areas where the most advanced thinking is likely to take place. With the freedom and openness now available to it, Protestantism has the opportunity to engage in creative thought and action to an almost unparalleled degree.

There are, to be sure, the inevitable dangers. The temptation is ever present for the church to become all things to all men. The temptation to power is still to be reckoned with, for it is just as great when power is absent as when power is present. Protestantism's theological confusion continues unabated, and all the exciting new programs for lay training and education have not yet begun to change the situation. The success of the churches in terms of money and property continues to inhibit their courage and imagination. Yet when the score is added up, it seems clear that contemporary American Protestantism has before it opportunities which equal any that it has enjoyed in the past. It remains to be seen how those opportunities will be used.

AUTHOR'S NOTES

INTRODUCTION

1. Winthrop Hudson, *The Great Tradition of the American Churches* (New York, 1963), p. 9. Hudson refers to the "carefully defined equilibrium of church and state," but a wider application of his striking phrase seems warranted.

2. Winthrop Hudson, *American Protestantism* (Chicago, 1961), contains a concise summation of these epochs and their effects on the churches.

3. Franklin H. Littell, *From State Church to Pluralism* (Garden City, 1962), p. x.

4. *Ibid.*, p. 32. Littell reports 6.9 per cent for 1800, 35.7 per cent for 1900.

5. Robert T. Handy, "The Protestant Search for a Christian America," *Church History*, Vol. XXII, No. 1 (March, 1953), p. 10.

1. THE EMERGENCE OF THE SECULAR STATE

1. See Carl Bridenbaugh, *Mitre and Sceptre* (New York, 1962), on which this account is based.
2. Anson Phelps Stokes, *Church and State in the United States,* Vol. I (New York, 1950), pp. 371-374.
3. *Ibid.,* pp. 432-439.
4. *Ibid.,* p. 602.
5. Quoted in *ibid.,* p. 609.
6. *Ibid.,* p. 537.
7. In 1965, however, this traditional stand was implicitly repudiated when the Catholic Council on Civil Liberties submitted to the United States Supreme Court an *amicus curiae* brief in the case of Griswold *v.* Connecticut which sought to have the Connecticut anti-contraceptive law declared unconstitutional on the ground that it constituted an improper invasion by government into an area which ought to remain within the private jurisdiction of the family. The Court's decision to void the law received general approbation in Roman Catholic circles. See the New York *Times,* June 8, 1965, p. 35. For a Catholic reaction, see *Commonweal,* Vol. LXXXII, No. 16 (July 9, 1965), p. 491.
8. Will Herberg, *Protestant-Catholic-Jew* (Garden City, 1960), pp. 74-78.
9. See the penetrating analysis of this issue in Sidney E. Mead, *The Lively Experiment* (New York, 1963), pp. 66-71.

2. POLITICS—AFTER THE GREAT CRUSADE

1. "Platform of Church Discipline," quoted in Thomas J. Wertenbaker, *The Puritan Oligarchy* (New York, 1947), p. 71.
2. New York *Times,* September 13, 1960.

3. FROM MISSION TO REALISM IN WORLD AFFAIRS

1. Ralph H. Gabriel, *The Course of American Democratic Thought* (New York, 1956), pp. 367-386.
2. Josiah Strong, *Expansion under New World Conditions* (New York, 1900), pp. 253-255.
3. Josiah Strong, *Our Country* (New York, 1885), pp. 176 ff.
4. Lyman Abbott, *The Rights of Man* (Boston, 1901), pp. 272-273.
5. Charles Olcott, *Life of William McKinley*, Vol. II (Boston, 1916), pp. 110-111; quoted in Frederick Merk, *Manifest Destiny and Mission in American History* (New York, 1963), p. 253.
6. George Hodges, *Henry Codman Potter* (New York, 1915), pp. 315 ff.
7. Washington Gladden, *Recollections* (Boston, 1909), p. 386.
8. Henry Churchill King, *President Wilson and the Moral Aims of the War*, p. 71; quoted in Ray H. Abrams, *Preachers Present Arms* (Washington, 1933), p. 50.
9. Randolph McKim, *For God and Country*, pp. 116-117; quoted in Abrams, *Preachers Present Arms*, p. 55.
10. *Christian Register*, Vol. XCVII (August 15, 1918), p. 775; quoted in Abrams, *Preachers Present Arms*, p. 68.
11. Paul A. Carter, *The Decline and Revival of the Social Gospel* (Ithaca, 1954), pp. 208 ff. This section relies on Carter's helpful interpretation.
12. *Ibid.*, p. 215.
13. *Ibid.*, p. 218.
14. Some of the principal arguments, pro and con, are summarized in Edwin Fogelman, *Hiroshima: The Decision to Use the A-Bomb* (New York, 1964).
15. See *ibid.*, pp. 75, 82 for the testimony of Japanese statesmen.
16. *Ibid.*, pp. 95-100. The American demand for "unconditional surrender" made it almost impossible to achieve a negotiated peace with Japan. Indications are that, had the Potsdam Declaration included a guarantee that the emperor would be retained, Japan's surrender could have been arranged long before the bombs were dropped.

17. Quoted in McGeorge Bundy, "Foreign Policy: From Innocence to Engagement," *Paths in American Thought,* ed. by Arthur M. Schlesinger, Jr., and Morton White (Boston, 1963), p. 305.
18. Samuel L. Sharp, "Political Realism and Christian Idealism," *Faculty Forum,* No. 26 (October, 1963), p. 1.

4. GODLINESS, THE SCHOOLS, AND THE AMERICAN CONSENSUS

1. Quoted in Anson Phelps Stokes, *Church and State in the United States,* Vol. II (New York, 1950), p. 57.
2. *Ibid.,* pp. 573-579.
3. Quoted in *ibid.,* p. 53.
4. Quoted in *ibid.,* pp. 520-521.
5. See Pennsylvania Humanities Commission, *Universal Issues in Human Life* (Harrisburg, 1965), for a well-thought-out curriculum.

5. THE ELUSIVE QUEST OF THE HIGHER LEARNING

1. Richard Hofstadter and C. DeWitt Hardy, *The Development and Scope of Higher Education in the United States* (New York, 1952), p. 3.
2. Frederick Rudolph, *The American College and University* (New York, 1962), pp. 13-14. This chapter relies heavily on Dr. Rudolph's excellent study.
3. Donald G. Tewksbury, *The Founding of American Colleges and Universities Before the Civil War* (New York, 1932), p. 151.
4. *Ibid.,* pp. 26-28.
5. Rudolph, *American College,* pp. 159-162.
6. Hofstadter and Hardy, *Development and Scope,* p. 119; Sylvanus M. Duvall, *The Methodist Episcopal Church and Education up to 1869* (New York, 1928), p. 111.
7. Rudolph, *American College,* pp. 131 ff.
8. Quoted in *ibid.,* p. 220.

9. Hofstadter and Hardy, *Development and Scope,* p. 32.

10. Rudolph, *American College,* p. 433.

11. Merrimon Cuninggim, *The Protestant Stake in Higher Education* (Washington, D.C., 1961), pp. 6-18.

12. Manning M. Pattillo and Donald M. MacKenzie, *Eight Hundred Colleges Face the Future* (St. Louis, 1965), p. 50.

13. *Ibid.,* pp. 23, 32.

14. *Ibid.,* p. 44.

15. *Ibid.,* pp. 20-22.

16. Guy E. Snavely, *The Church and the Four-Year College* (New York, 1955), p. 1.

17. Waldemar O. Doescher, *The Church College in Today's Culture* (Minneapolis, 1963), p. 38.

18. Pattillo and MacKenzie, *Eight Hundred Colleges,* pp. 51-52.

19. *Ibid.,* p. 59.

20. *Ibid.,* pp. 55-56.

21. *Ibid.,* pp. 60-61.

22. *Ibid.,* p. 55.

23. C. Grey Austin, *A Century of Religion at the University of Michigan* (Ann Arbor, 1957), pp. 3, 16.

24. Clarence P. Shedd, *The Church Follows Its Students* (New Haven, 1938), p. 13.

25. *Ibid.,* pp. 14-16.

26. Arnold S. Nash, *The University and the Modern World* (New York, 1943), p. 28.

27. Hofstadter and Hardy, *Development and Scope,* pp. 227, 233.

28. Nash, *The University,* p. 287.

29. *Ibid.,* p. 28.

30. Hofstadter and Hardy, *Development and Scope,* p. 103.

6. THE DEVELOPMENT OF A PROTESTANT SOCIAL CONSCIENCE

1. W. W. Rostow, *The Stages of Economic Growth* (Cambridge, Eng., 1963), pp. 4-10, 70-72.

2. Henry F. May, *Protestant Churches and Industrial America* (New York, 1949), p. 17. The early portion of this chapter is based largely on May's important study.

3. *Independent,* November 26, 1874, p. 14; quoted in May, *Protestant Churches,* p. 54.

4. *Congregationalist,* July 25, 1877, p. 236; quoted in May, *Protestant Churches,* p. 93.

5. *Christian Union,* August 1, 1877, p. 93; quoted in May, *Protestant Churches,* p. 94.

6. May, *Protestant Churches,* pp. 173-174.

7. *Ibid.,* p. 140.

8. *Social Aspects of Christianity* (New York, 1889), pp. 97-98; quoted in May, *Protestant Churches,* p. 141.

9. *Social Aspects of Christianity,* pp. 63 ff.; quoted in Charles Howard Hopkins, *The Rise of the Social Gospel in American Protestantism* (New Haven, 1940), p. 106.

10. May, *Protestant Churches,* pp. 163, 170, 235-236; cf. Paul A. Carter, *The Decline and Revival of the Social Gospel* (Ithaca, 1954), pp. 12-13.

11. *Dawn,* July-August, 1890, p. 111; quoted in May, *Protestant Churches,* p. 243.

12. Hopkins, *Rise of the Social Gospel,* p. 189.

13. *Ibid.,* pp. 114-115.

14. *Ibid.,* pp. 280-296.

15. Harry F. Ward, *The Social Creed of the Churches* (New York, 1914), pp. 5-8.

16. Hopkins, *Rise of the Social Gospel,* pp. 313-314.

17. Winthrop Hudson, *The Great Tradition of the American Churches* (New York, 1963), pp. 186-194.

18. Hopkins, *Rise of the Social Gospel,* pp. 124-125. The reference is to Philip S. Moxom, *The Religion of Hope* (Boston, 1896), p. 66.

19. Hopkins, *Rise of the Social Gospel,* pp. 125, 220-221.

20. Hudson, *Great Tradition,* pp. 226-242. This interpretation is based on Hudson's sensitive essay on Rauschenbusch.

21. Carter, *Decline and Revival,* p. 34.

22. *Ibid.,* p. 38.

23. Donald B. Meyer, *The Protestant Search for Political Realism* (Berkeley, 1961), p. 122.

24. *Ibid.,* pp. 107-117.

25. Carter, *Decline and Revival,* pp. 125-126.

26. *Ibid.,* pp. 60-68.

27. *Ibid.,* p. 133.
28. *Ibid.,* p. 145.
29. See Reinhold Niebuhr, "Intellectual Autobiography of Reinhold Niebuhr," in *Reinhold Niebuhr: His Religious, Social and Political Thought,* edited by Charles W. Kegley and Robert W. Bretall (New York, 1961), pp. 1-23, for Niebuhr's own evaluation of his life and work.
30. Reinhold Niebuhr, *The Nature and Destiny of Man,* Vol. I (New York, 1964), p. 18.
31. Niebuhr, "Intellectual Autobiography," p. 13.

7. THE URBAN MISSION COMES OF AGE

1. Morton G. White and Lucia White, *The Intellectual versus the City* (Cambridge, Mass., 1962).
2. Quoted in J. H. Plumb, *England in the Eighteenth Century* (Harmondsworth, 1950), p. 97.
3. William R. Hutchison, *The Transcendentalist Ministers* (New Haven, 1959), pp. 157-163.
4. A. I. Abell, *The Urban Impact on American Protestantism* (Hamden, 1962), p. 30. Professor Abell's study is by far the most valuable for the early years of this movement and has been used extensively in preparing this chapter.
5. *Ibid.,* pp. 147-150.
6. *Ibid.,* p. 149.
7. Quoted in *ibid.,* pp. 162-163.
8. *Ibid.,* p. 164.
9. *Ibid.,* p. 182.
10. *Ibid.,* p. 121 n.
11. W. W. Rostow, *The Stages of Economic Growth* (Cambridge, Eng., 1963), pp. 79-80.
12. Perry L. Norton, *Church and Metropolis* (New York, 1964), p. 24. A Standard Metropolitan Statistical Area is defined as an area having an urban center with a population of 50,000 or more and a population density in the surrounding area of 150 persons per square mile.

13. Truman B. Douglass, "The Job the Protestants Shirk," in *Cities and Churches,* ed. by Robert Lee (Philadelphia, 1962), p. 87.

14. *Ibid.,* p. 88.

15. *Ibid.,* pp. 87-88.

16. George W. Webber, *God's Colony in Man's World* (Nashville, 1960), pp. 15-16.

17. Ross W. Sanderson, *The Church Serves the Changing City* (New York, 1955), p. 195.

18. For a full account of the East Harlem Protestant Parish, see Webber, *God's Colony.*

19. *Ibid.,* pp. 28-29.

20. Sanderson, *Church Serves,* pp. 89 ff.; Paul Moore, Jr., *The Church Reclaims the City* (New York, 1964). See esp. Mrs. Moore's chapter, "The Clergyman's Family in the Inner City," pp. 200-210.

21. Moore, p. 28; Walter Kloetzli, *The Church and the Urban Challenge* (Philadelphia, 1961), p. 76.

22. Moore, *Church Reclaims,* p. 10.

23. Paul Musselman, *The Church on the Urban Frontier* (New York, 1960), p. 6.

24. Walter Kloetzli and Arthur Hillman, *Urban Church Planning* (Philadelphia, 1958), p. 159.

25. Joseph Sittler, "Urban Fact and the Human Situation," *Challenge and Response in the City,* ed. by Walter Kloetzli (Rock Island, 1962), p. 12.

26. *Ibid.,* p. 13.

27. Norton, *Church and Metropolis,* pp. 85-86.

28. Gibson Winter, *The Suburban Captivity of the Churches* (Garden City, 1961), p. 170.

29. See esp. Harvey Cox, *The Secular City* (New York, 1965), pp. 38-58.

30. J. V. Langmead Casserley, "Children of God in the City of Man," in *Cities and Churches,* p. 63.

31. Peter L. Berger, "Community in Modern Urban Society," in *Cities and Churches,* p. 68.

32. Gibson Winter, *The New Creation as Metropolis* (New York, 1963), p. 2.

33. Winter, *Suburban Captivity,* p. 74.

8. THE PERSISTENT PERPLEXITY OF RACE

1. Daniel Boorstin, *The Lost World of Thomas Jefferson,* Beacon paperback ed. (Boston, 1960), pp. 88-98.

2. Louis Filler, *The Crusade against Slavery* (New York, 1960), p. 15.

3. Kyle Haselden, *The Racial Problem in Christian Perspective* (New York, 1964), p. 30.

4. *Ibid.,* pp. 30-31.

5. C. Vann Woodward, *The Strange Career of Jim Crow* (New York, 1957), pp. 15 ff.

6. Franz Boas's anthropological studies around the turn of the century were probably the most significant single influence on American social science, though racist theories can hardly be said to have been generally abandoned by the social scientists until the 1920's. See Gunnar Myrdal, *An American Dilemma,* 20th anniversary ed. (New York, 1962), pp. 90-93.

SELECTED BIBLIOGRAPHY

Abbott, Lyman. *The Rights of Man.* Boston: Houghton Mifflin Co., 1901.

Abell, Aaron I. *The Urban Impact on American Protestantism.* Hamden: Archon Press, 1962.

Abrams, Ray H. *Preachers Present Arms.* Washington: Round Table Press, 1933.

Austin, C. Grey. *A Century of Religion at the University of Michigan.* Ann Arbor (?), 1957.

Berger, Peter L. *The Noise of Solemn Assemblies.* Garden City: Doubleday & Co., 1961.

Boorstin, Daniel. *The Lost World of Thomas Jefferson.* Beacon Paperback Edition. Boston: Beacon Press, 1950.

Bridenbaugh, Carl. *Mitre and Sceptre.* New York: Oxford University Press, 1962.

Cantelon, John E. *A Protestant Approach to the Campus Ministry.* Philadelphia: Westminster Press, 1964.

Carter, Paul A. *The Decline and Revival of the Social Gospel.* Ithaca: Cornell University Press, 1954.

239

Cass, James and Birnbaum, Max. *Comparative Guide to American Colleges.* New York: Harper & Row, 1964.

Childs, Marquis W. and Cater, Douglass. *Ethics in a Business Society.* New York: New American Library of World Literature, 1954.

Cogley, John (ed.). *Religion in America.* New York: Meridian Books, 1958.

Commager, Henry S. *The American Mind.* New Haven: Yale University Press, 1950.

Cox, Harvey. *The Secular City.* New York: The Macmillan Co., 1965.

Cuninggim, Merrimon. *The Protestant Stake in Higher Education.* Washington, D.C.: Council of Protestant Colleges and Universities, 1961.

Doescher, Waldemar. *The Church College in Today's Culture.* Minneapolis: Augsburg Publishing House, 1963.

Filler, Louis. *The Crusade against Slavery.* New York: Harper & Row, 1960.

Fogelman, Edwin. *Hiroshima: The Decision to Use the A-Bomb.* New York: Charles Scribner's Sons, 1964.

Gabriel, Ralph H. *The Course of American Democratic Thought.* 2nd ed.; New York: Ronald Press, 1956.

Gladden, Washington. *Recollections.* Boston: Houghton Mifflin Co., 1909.

Handy, Robert T. "The Protestant Search for a Christian America," *Church History,* XXII (March, 1953), 8-19.

Haselden, Kyle. *The Racial Problem in Christian Perspective.* New York: Harper & Row, 1964.

Herberg, Will. *Protestant-Catholic-Jew.* Garden City: Doubleday & Co., 1960.

Hodges, George. *Henry Codman Potter.* New York: The Macmillan Co., 1915.

Hofstadter, Richard. *Social Darwinism in American Thought.* Rev. ed.; Boston: Beacon Press, 1955.

Hofstadter, Richard and Hardy, C. DeWitt. *The Development and Scope of Higher Education in the United States.* New York: Columbia University Press, 1952.

Hopkins, Charles Howard. *The Rise of the Social Gospel in American Protestantism.* New Haven: Yale University Press, 1940.

Hudson, Winthrop. *American Protestantism.* Chicago: University of Chicago Press, 1961.

————. *The Great Tradition of the American Churches.* New York: Harper & Row, 1963.

Hutchison, William R. *The Transcendentalist Ministers.* New Haven: Yale University Press, 1959.

Kegley, Charles W. and Bretall, Robert W. *Reinhold Niebuhr: His Religious, Social and Political Thought.* New York: The Macmillan Co., 1961.

Kerr, Clark. *The Uses of the University.* Cambridge, Mass.: Harvard University Press, 1963.

Kloetzli, Walter. *Challenge and Response in the City.* Rock Island: Augustana Press, 1962.

————. *The Church and the Urban Challenge.* Philadelphia: Muhlenberg Press, 1961.

Kloetzli, Walter and Hillman, Arthur. *Urban Church Planning.* Philadelphia: Muhlenberg Press, 1958.

Lee, Robert (ed.). *Cities and Churches.* Philadelphia: Westminster Press, 1962.

Lenski, Gerhard. *The Religious Factor.* Garden City: Doubleday & Co., 1961.

Littell, Franklin H. *From State Church to Pluralism.* Garden City: Doubleday & Co., 1962.

Marty, Martin E. *The New Shape of American Religion.* New York: Harper & Row, 1959.

————. "The Protestant Reinterpretation of American Life," *The Outbursts That Await Us.* Edited by Arthur Hertzberg. New York: The Macmillan Co., 1963.

May, Henry F. *Protestant Churches and Industrial America.* New York: Harper & Row, 1949.

Mead, Sidney E. *The Lively Experiment.* New York: Harper & Row, 1963.

Merk, Frederick. *Manifest Destiny and Mission in American History.* New York: Alfred A. Knopf, 1963.

Meyer, Donald B. *The Protestant Search for Political Realism.* Berkeley: University of California Press, 1961.

Miller, Alexander. *Faith and Learning*. New York: Association Press, 1960.

Miller, William Lee. *The Protestant and Politics*. Philadelphia: Westminster Press, 1958.

Moore, Paul, Jr. *The Church Reclaims the City*. New York: Seabury Press, 1964.

Musselman, G. Paul. *The Church on the Urban Frontier*. New York: Seabury Press, 1960.

Myrdal, Gunnar. *An American Dilemma*. 20th anniversary ed.; New York: Harper & Row, 1962.

Nash, Arnold S. *The University and the Modern World*. New York: The Macmillan Co., 1943.

Niebuhr, H. Richard. *The Kingdom of God in America*. Harper Torchbook; New York: Harper & Row, 1959.

————. *The Social Sources of Denominationalism*. New York: Meridian Books, 1958.

Niebuhr, Reinhold. *The Nature and Destiny of Man*. Scribner Library ed.; 2 Vols. New York: Charles Scribner's Sons, 1964.

Norton, Perry L. *Church and Metropolis*. New York: Seabury Press, 1964.

Olmstead, Clifton E. *Religion in America, Past and Present*. Englewood Cliffs: Prentice-Hall, 1961.

Pattillo, Manning, Jr. and MacKenzie, Donald M. *Eight Hundred Colleges Face the Future*. St. Louis, Danforth Foundation, 1965.

Raab, Earl (ed.). *Religious Conflict in America*. Garden City: Doubleday & Co., 1964.

Riesman, David. *Constraint and Variety in American Education*. Garden City: Doubleday & Co., 1958.

Rostow, W. W. *The Stages of Economic Growth*. Cambridge, Eng.: Cambridge University Press, 1963.

Rudolph, Frederick. *The American College and University*. New York: Alfred A. Knopf, 1962.

Sanderson, Ross W. *The Church Serves the Changing City*. New York: Harper & Row, 1955.

Schlesinger, Arthur M., Jr., and White, Morton (eds.). *Paths in American Thought*. Boston: Houghton Mifflin Co., 1963.

Schneider, Herbert W. *Religion in Twentieth Century America.* Cambridge, Mass.: Harvard University Press, 1952.

Sharp, Samuel L. "Political Realism and Christian Idealism," *Faculty Forum,* No. 26 (October, 1963), pp. 1-2.

Shedd, Clarence P. *The Church Follows Its Students.* New Haven: Yale University Press, 1938.

Snavely, Guy. *The Church and the Four Year College.* New York: Harper & Row, 1955.

Stedman, Murray S., Jr. *Religion and Politics in America.* New York: Harcourt, Brace & World, 1964.

Stokes, Anson Phelps. *Church and State in the United States.* 3 Vols. New York: Harper & Row, 1950.

Strong, Josiah. *Expansion under New World Conditions.* New York: Baker & Taylor Co., 1900.

————. *Our Country.* New York: The American Home Missionary Society, 1885.

Tewksbury, Donald G. *The Founding of American Colleges and Universities before the Civil War.* New York: Teachers College, Columbia, 1932.

Thompson, Kenneth W. *Christian Ethics and the Dilemmas of Foreign Policy.* Durham: Duke University Press, 1959.

Ward, Harry F. *The Social Creed of the Churches.* New York: Eaton & Mains, 1914.

Webber, George W. *God's Colony in Man's World.* Nashville: Abingdon Press, 1960.

Wertenbaker, Thomas J. *The Puritan Oligarchy.* New York: Grosset & Dunlap, 1947.

White, Morton G. and White, Lucia. *The Intellectual versus the City.* Cambridge, Mass.: Harvard University Press and the M. I. T. Press, 1962.

Winter, Gibson. *The New Creation as Metropolis.* New York: The Macmillan Co., 1963.

————. *The Suburban Captivity of the Churches.* Garden City: Doubleday & Co., 1961.

Woodward, C. Vann. *The Strange Career of Jim Crow.* New York: Oxford University Press, 1957.

INDEX